Planning for Survival

The Great Retirement Conundrum

Jay H. Levy, CFP®, CRPC® CPRC™

JHL Publishing

STRATHAM, NEW HAMPSHIRE

Jay H. Levy/JHL Publishing
32 Dumbarton Oaks
Stratham, NH 03885
jaylevyplanning.net
jaylevyplanning@gmail.com

Planning to Survive/ Jay H. Levy. -- 1st ed.
ISBN 978-1-7350132-0-6

This book is dedicated to my family. To my two sons, Adam, and Grant, who from the very beginning have provided years of joy—feelings which have continued as I've observed you becoming fine young men of which two parents could not be prouder. Your love and continued growth as individuals inspire us to stick around if possible, to be part of your journey.

To Linda Horsager, who is the matriarch of such a great clan comprised of multiple generations thank you. My greatest fortune has been in becoming part of your family.

I also want to especially remember my father-in-law, Les Horsager, who taught me through his daily life, the importance and joy of becoming genuinely interested in people, regardless of who they are. It was a lesson that I observed almost immediately more than thirty years ago and one that has had a profound impact on my life.

To the rest of the Horsager clan including Jeff, Shannon, William, and Griffin Horsager, Drs. Robyn and James Boehrer, Dr. Alexander Boehrer and Katherine Boehrer, you are all wonderful. I also want to acknowledge my brother Kim and his wife Ruth; my nephews Mike, Jonathan, and Dr. Jason Levy; my brother-in-law Robert and Cindy Chaikin and nieces Jara McDermott and Dr. Nicole Chaikin.

Thank you to my deceased parents Richard and Mildred Levy, along with deceased siblings Brian Levy and Donna Chaikin. I wish you could all be here to read and absorb a few of these life lessons that were formulated from the family dynamics I experienced in the early years.

To Renee Levy, who inspires me with the passion and energy of staying unretired as a way of continuing to remain alive, healthy, and relevant for eighty-seven years (and counting).

To my many clients, friends and associates over the years from whom I've learned so much –through all the challenges, disappointments, and the celebrations, I treasure the life lessons I've learned from each and every one of you.

The most important thanks belong to the love of my life, my wife, Kelly. For more than thirty years, you have been the person I've most respected and admired—in your career, as the matriarch of our family, a tireless runner 365 days a year and most importantly, a petite woman with the big heart. It is my hope that with continued planning, good health, and a pinch of luck, we will have another half-century together.

"When I was young, I used to think that money was the most important thing in life. Now that I am old, I know it is."

Oscar Wilde

Contents

Acknowledgements

I'd like to thank all of the colleagues, past and present who I've had the pleasure of working with over the years including; Edward Benway, Deb Curtis, Melinda Anthony, Steve Bruno CFA, Ted Shediac, Tim Hamilton, Ken Groppi, Kyle Powers, Michael Fung CFA, David Batchelder CFA, and Kelly Foss Root.

A special thanks goes to Fred Forman Esq., who has shared his expertise in estate planning. This area has become an integral part of the overall financial planning circle that I have worked with many clients to develop.

To so many at TD Ameritrade who provide custodian services to safeguard all assets that we manage. Their technology advances have made our lives significantly more effective and streamlined.

To Dan Ziabatis of John Hancock, Jeff Meade of Fidelity, Steve Naber of TD Ameritrade, Amy Madden,

Allianz Life, thank you for your continued support. I truly appreciate all you do.

To Scott and Leslie Carson, Dana Fainery, Jackie Eastwood, Sheila Miller, Dr. Babu Ramdev, a special shout-out of gratitude for sharing personal insights regarding various topics ranging from education, medical, and even past histories. Your insights provided valuable guidance to what the future may look like. To so many at Horsesmouth who have provided years of invaluable education and guidance including Elaine Floyd CFP; Debra Taylor CPA/PFS, JD, CDFA; Jeff Levine CPA/PPS, CFP, CWS, MSA; Chris Holman, and Sean Bailey.

I am so grateful to Tim Barber and Grant Levy for their creative processes in developing a book cover design that is elegant and clean, yet powerful. It was vastly different from my original version and now in hindsight, so much better.

To Kelly and Mike Lydick for their work in the copy-editing process of ensuring that this book was properly structured to read more fluidly.

Thank you, Kelly Levy for your technical guidance throughout this process. Your computer support and problem solving proved invaluable.

Charlie Epstein (A/K/A) is The 401k Coach whose knowledge and insights into the defined contribution benefits world have provided years of guidance and education. Charlie's gentle push for writing and getting published certainly did not hurt this project!

Thank you to David Horsager, author of the best-selling *Trust Edge* who has developed a permanent message that continually influences and inspires me to this day to always place other people first. David certainly was one of the key people that unwittingly provided inspiration for my writing this book. Additionally, a special thanks to his brother, Kent Horsager, for his guidance and willingness over the years to engage in discussions surrounding defensive-minded investment strategies.

Additionally, I want to give a special thanks to the many other friends, mentors, and acquaintances who I have had the gift of having in my life over the years. I have certainly learned more from them than they have from me. They include Gary and Jamie Goodman, Craig and Karen Gendron (I've enjoyed the FINRA conversations over the years), Rich Middleton, Dr. Maureen Sullivan, John and Mary Lyons, Diane Gentempo, Carol and John Hazekamp, Jon and Donna Huot, Tim and Michelle Tetreault, Nathan Hale and Jamie Flaws,

Maureen and Mark Raiche, Dr. Babu Ramdev, Don and Kathy Larnard, Jeff and Melissa Foy, Jeff and Barbara Hughes, Carol Bailey, Greg Walker, Peter Walcek, Jeff Pollock, Ellen Caille, Mike Carella, Tom Torr, Anne Jamieson, John Salmon, Tony James, Roger Hamel, Dr. Peter Dirksmeier, Dr. Bill Hassett, Dr. Anne Kalter, Dr. Paul Cass, Dr. Marcela Del Carmen, Mike Bolduc, ESQ, Dr. Terri Lally, James Brannen, Ingo Roemer, Dr. Andrew Warshaw, Dr. Roger Evans, Chad Kageleiry, Tom Levasseur, Geofrey Ness, Larry Raiche, CPA, Dr. Alison Sollee, Michael Steinberg, Dave Verno, Ann and Frank Torr, Rick and Sue Card, Doreen and Greg Crisp, Clayton and Cheryl Currier, Joel and Paula Degenaars, Chris and Betsy Wolf, Dana Ferniany, Betty Beathard, Cindy and David Francis, Mark Galvin, Ken and Judy George, Christi and Michael Hassel Shearer, David and Lisa Horsager, Kent and Beth Horsager, Sandia and David Wasserman, Governor Tim and Mary Pawlenty, Maureen Raiche, John Rivard CPA, Doug and Stella Scammon, Steve Scott, Amy Schwartz, Todd and Christine Sigmon, Dr. Geoff and Kelly Starr, Mark and Shauna Troy, Karen and Denny Zaun, Todd and Kyoko Zaun, Mary and Clarence Horsager, and the late Senator John McCain.

To the countless number of other of people who I've had the pleasure of interacting with over the years at the Wentworth Douglass Hospital and Foundation, thank you for the incredible amount of knowledge and caring that you showed our community in making the Seacoast a healthier community.

And last, but certainly not least, a very special thanks to Erin Tamberella, who through my good fortune of connecting with her through Horsesmouth, was extremely instrumental in working to fine tune my writing, to condense the content into a readable format, and generally act as the head coach in the drafting, editing, design and overall journey which we lovingly refer to as the publication process. Looking forward to teaming together on the next book!

Preface

As I sat at my computer on March 18, 2020, my thoughts raced wildly with concerns over events I never could have imagined in my lifetime. While always steadfast in my commentary to clients on holding the course and putting market volatility into perspective, at that moment, I found myself at a loss.

And no, it had nothing to do with the prior day's announcement that New England Patriots quarterback, Tom Brady, had decided to take his talents down to Tampa Bay. On any normal day in New England, this kind of news would have driven the masses to stockpile anti-depressants.

It also had nothing to do with another Boston legend, Mookie Betts, being traded to the Los Angeles Dodgers. No, those stories would have been a welcome relief—except that by March 18, 2020, normal distractions from sports on television was nonexistent. No NBA, NHL, tennis, golf, or even MLB. All were put on temporary and potentially permanent hiatus due to a coronavirus now forever known as COVID-19.

To say that globally, our day-to-day reality has changed, would be the understatement of a lifetime. Common everyday activities such as travel, cruises, restaurants, bars, casinos, have either been suspended, closed, or severely curtailed as communities and countries around the world scramble to keep the virus contained. To protect the healthcare infrastructure from becoming overwhelmed, containment efforts have extended from social distancing protocol to mandatory self-quarantine.

Causes for the 2008 Great Recession were primarily due to manmade financial creations such as the risky mortgage-backed securities that plagued the world at the time. This, in turn, resulted in an economic crisis that set the world on edge and destroyed a significant amount of wealth. All of this put many people out of work and caused many businesses to close.

The COVID-19 crisis, on the other hand, is a healthcare issue that as of the date of this writing will certainly lead to an economic crisis, and potentially, a financial one as well. Market volatility has been unprecedented with days of seeing a 10% correction happening far too frequently. Over a three-week span from late February to mid-March, equity markets lost an astounding 30-35%. This has never occurred—even during the Great Depression.

Those seeking relief from fixed income markets have also been stymied, as evidenced by the fall of the 10-year U.S Treasury to a shocking 0.30 basis point level. Massive monetary policies from the Fed and fiscal action from the U.S Government are in full force as Americans prepare to face unprecedented employment loss.

Small and mid-size businesses are closing. We could possibly see the potential collapse of whole industries including airlines, automobile, energy, to name a few. Over the last four weeks, we have witnessed an economic domino effect few could have imagined in such a short period of time.

During the September 11, 2001, terrorist attack, there was eventually an identifiable culprit to pursue which gave people a level of comfort as they went about their everyday activities. While short-term, many people had reservations about flying or traveling abroad, they were always able to congregate, enjoy restaurants and the social diversions that sports, concerts, and movies provided.

As of March 2020, the new mantra is isolation at home for an unknown period. We are hoping for one to two months, but no one really knows for sure. If there is one thing the markets hate, it is uncertainty, and uncertainty is running rampant at the moment.

My manuscript for this book was completed before we knew Corona as anything more than that beer you put a lime into. Although not originally part of the book, I decided to include this preface as a sort of "an intro to my intro."

While the book was moving through the editing process, several people commented that I had great foresight to address the current situation in my new book. As I explained to people, that the book had nothing to do with the virus, I came to realize that it had everything to do with the virus. The virus was simply a trigger that has caused both individuals and businesses to assess where they stand financially throughout an emergency.

While a health crisis trigger is not anyone's fault, the failure to properly have planned for such unforeseen "emergencies" is. This book helps you to lay a foundation of proper planning. It is this type of planning that can prepare you for all the curve balls life has a way of throwing over one's journey.

This book helps you build a wall of self-preservation against any kind of potentially life-changing "trigger." This includes job loss, changes in a family dynamic (birth of a child or taking financial responsibility for an ailing family member), dealing with a significant health issue, and even working to build an income stream that gives you the freedom of having options. Depending on your individual lifestyle, these may include options for retiring, scaling back, or even changing careers and finding more satisfying work.

One of the key points that I hope you can take from this book is that these so-called "triggers" can and do occur over everyone's lifetime. Hopefully, this fact will become clear from introduction to the conclusion.

Ultimately, I came to realize that so much of what I have presented in this book is, indeed, applicable to the current situation that is happening. I have peppered the book with true stories of what I have seen and some of the challenges I have helped people through over the course of my career. Hopefully, you will find the book both very readable and relatable.

It is imperative that people, regardless of age, read this book, so they fully appreciate that the decisions made today can have longer term consequences down the road. These may be positive or negative, financial, or emotional. Regardless, it is always wise to be prepared and that takes a lifetime of proper planning, which is what this book is all about.

Regardless of when you commence reading this book, I am hopeful that the COVID-19 events will be under control or even better—in the rear-view mirror. What life after COVID-19 will look like for countries around the world remains to seen. However, the importance of learning good habits and planning will never be more relevant than it is today. Stay healthy and good reading.

Introduction

This is a book about the importance of planning for your financial future, but it is about so much more. I have been in the financial industry for more than thirty years and in that time, I have seen it all—the good, the bad, and the ugly. I have worked with all kinds of people from different walks of life, and I have learned many valuable financial and life lessons along the way.

My goal in this book is to educate, motivate, and inspire you to act and delay gratification today, so you can enjoy the tomorrow you have always dreamed of. I have seen firsthand, the consequences of inaction, and nothing demonstrates this lesson better than the story of someone very dear to me.

Donna Mimi Chaikin died on August 3, 2019 at the age of 74. She was the daughter of Richard and Mildred Levy, and she was also was my sister.

By all accounts, Donna did not have the easiest of childhoods. When WWII ended, her father, Richard, ruled his first child with somewhat of an iron fist. As other families enjoyed the prosperity of a postwar life, Richard was much more conservative with his family's budget. He had been a primary breadwinner for his divorced mother and younger brother since the age of 13. This upbringing resulted in an extremely frugal discipline with his own family.

As fortunes boomed during the 1950s, birthrates soared, and consumption rose dramatically. However, it was a very different story for Donna. Although she did not live a life of poverty, her memories of childhood were dominated by thoughts of everything she *did not* have. As classmates enjoyed family trips to New York and new clothes, Donna's recollections are consumed by all the things she had wanted but was refused.

She went on to some post-secondary schooling, but never went to college. Other than working as a low-level assistant in New York's fashion district, she had no real career path prior to marriage. In her mid-twenties, she met a handsome Jewish dentist and they were married soon thereafter. Mom was happy because she married "a nice Jewish boy." Her father was thrilled with her choice because he was from the same religious faith, had been in the military, and most importantly, could support his daughter.

Life seemed perfect for the first ten years of Donna's marriage. With her helping administratively, the dentist opened a couple of offices and they enjoyed a healthy income. It would not be long before two beautiful daughters came into the world. Donna was finally living the high life.

Over time, Donna's father began to lecture her husband about spending, trying to persuade him to avoid giving into her every whim. This only drove Donna to live a more extravagant lifestyle. She insisted that her children attend the best private schools, take piano lessons, and, of course, they joined the local country club. The curious thing about Donna's new lifestyle was it did not seem to make her happy. In fact, quite the opposite.

Increasingly more often, she flaunted her materialism as some dysfunctional payback to her father for his alleged failures in her childhood. This began her downward spiral and over time, people began to avoid her in social circles. Her husband fell out of love with her and her family began to distance themselves from her. It was not long before she fell into excessive drinking, prescription drugs, depression, suicide attempts, and, finally, divorce.

The years went by and the money ran out. Medicare became Medicaid and she eventually died a lonely, broken woman. The most heartbreaking part of all is that her situation could have been avoided. One of Donna's primary problems was she had no real purpose in her life. She had no charitable inclinations, and certainly no interest in exploring employment opportunities that might have peaked a long-forgotten passion or buried interest.

Prior to the finalization of her divorce, I had a conversation with my sister—a conversation that could have changed her life. One night after dinner with family, we went back to my home where Donna continued her "woe is me" routine. I asked everyone to leave the room while I sat with her. I quietly but directly explained that she was at a crossroads in her life. I soon discovered an underlying problem. Her complete identity hinged on her being part of a family unit. I remember wondering if the individual Donna Chaikin could survive or ever be "happy."

I thought it was important in her journey to find something—anything—that could help her discover some sort of passion in her life. It could have been religious, volunteering for a cause, or working in an interesting job. The latter offered the additional benefit of giving her an opportunity to build a nest egg for later years. It might also have helped her develop a new social network of friends and even build her self-confidence.

Unfortunately, when Donna arrived at her fork in the road, the choice she made was one of self-destruction. It takes effort to rise above all the personal baggage you have acquired since birth. Donna made the decision to not even try.

As tragic as my sister's life may appear, her time should not be written off as insignificant. It was Donna's story, along with many others I have encountered over the years, that prompted me to write this book. These stories of what people did or failed to do at critical junctures in their lives are designed to teach. By sharing these stories, if just one person (or millions) learn that there are always consequences to one's actions or inactions, then my effort was well worth it.

You see, Americans have a big problem. The U.S. is at a crossroads—one that could change the very fabric of society. Every day the media reports on the growing divergence between the "haves" and "have nots." Just as I never dreamed, we would be self-quarantining in this country during the Coronavirus, I also could have never imagined a time in this country when political debates centered around a path from capitalism to socialism.

An October 24, 2019, *The Wall Street Journal* ran a story on the Texas capital of Austin and how the city was forced to face its homelessness epidemic. Compared to other major metropolitan areas such as Los Angeles, San Francisco, or Seattle, Austin's homeless numbers did not jump off the page. However, the estimated point-in-time count of 2014 had grown an estimated 30% over five years.[1]

The growing problem resulted in heated discussions on how the crisis could be handled in a more humane and efficient manner. While the absolute number, a little over a 2,000 homeless in a population of 1.2M seems minute, it was a crisis in the making.[2]

The homeless problem not only infects the desirability of living in a area, but subsequently, home and rental prices, business formation, and health issues. As homeless numbers balloon, it becomes increasingly more common for residents, tourists, and business owners avoiding sidewalk tents, needles, feces, growing crime, and more.

So, what does that have to do with a book on planning? Everything!

Another *Wall Street Journal* article highlighted how the historic asset boom (10-year recovery since the Great Recession) passed half of All-American families by. This bottom half of all U.S. households have only recently regained the wealth they lost from the 2007-2009

---

[1] Elizabeth Findell. "Homelessness Becomes More Visible In Austin, Sparking Political Clash." *Wall Street Journal*. October 24, 2019. https://www.wsj.com/articles/homeless-becomes-more-visible-in-austin-sparking-political-clash-11571914802

[2] Ibid.

recession.[3] Even after all this time, they still have 32% less wealth (AFI) than in 2003.[4] Comparatively speaking, the top 1% of households have more than twice as much as they did in 2003.[5]

Why the discrepancy? It appears that the bottom 50% have most of their net worth (assets minus liabilities) in their home (assuming they own one).[6] However, the top 1% have an estimated 85% of their net worth in stocks, bonds, or stakes in private companies.[7]

Remember that net worth is very different than income. Economic and regulatory trends over the past decade have favored stocks over owning a home, making it ironically, more difficult for the less affluent to buy a home. Home ownership has fallen from 43% in 2007 to 37% in 2016.[8]

What does that have to do with a book on planning? Everything.

When we examine generational concerns, it only makes sense to start with the Baby Boomers. A 2018 Retirement Confidence Survey by the Employee Benefit

---

[3] David Harrison. "Historical Asset Boom Passes By Half of Families." *Wall Street Journal.* August 30, 2019. https://www.wsj.com/articles/historic-asset-boom-passes-by-half-of-families-11567157400

[4] Ibid.

[5] Ibid.

[6] Ibid.

[7] Ibid.

[8] Ibid.

Research Institute and the independent research firm, Greenwald and Associates, showed that those born between 1946-1964 are retiring at a rate estimated to be 10,000 per day for the next 10 years.[9]

The survey also found that 45% of workers report a total value of their household savings and investments less than $25,000 which would not begin to cover an adult 65 years or older who spends an average of $48,885 a year.[10] Additional research by the Insured Retirement Institute also supports trouble on the Baby Boomer horizon with 45% of the Baby Boomers having no retirement savings and of the remaining 55% who do, 28% of them have less than $100,000.[11] This translates into almost 50% of retirees depending on their Social Security benefits almost exclusively to live in retirement.[12]

What does this have to do with a book on planning? Everything.

Let us go a little younger in the generational chart! The 2018 Pew Research Center reflects that 29% live in "lower class" households which is comprised of a median

---

[9] "Retirement Confidence Survey." *Employee Benefit Research Institute.* April 24, 2018. https://www.ebri.org/docs/default-source/rcs/1_2018rcs_report_v5mgachecked.pdf?sfvrsn=e2e9302f_2
[10] Ibid.
[11] David Hass. "Retirement Trends of Baby Boomers, *Forbes,* September 3, 2019. https://www.forbes.com/sites/forbesfinancecouncil/2019/09/03/retirement-trends-of-baby-boomers/#4fa6a60d7378
[12] Ibid.

income of $25,624.[13] Lower class is defined as household income less than two-thirds of the national median (after income has been adjusted for household size).[14] More than 52% of households are considered middle class (median income of $78,442 in 2016) while 19% are upper class (median income of $187,872 in 2016).[15] While there is no disputing a growing gap between the middle and the upper class over the last decade, recent social versus capitalistic sparring is less likely to provide any effective resolution in improving such circumstances.

What does this have to do with a book on planning? Everything.

I believe there is a real need for a book like this. Let us face it. When it comes to financial acumen, most Americans are relatively uneducated. This is evidenced by statistics regarding financial preparedness. What this book will do is guide you through your financial life cycle. I will be your guide and mentor as I point out important issues you should know at each stage of your financial

---

[13] Kathleen Elkins. "29% of Americans Are Considered Lower Class - Here is How Much Money They Earn." *CNBC.* September 28, 2019. https://www.cnbc.com/2019/09/28/how-much-the-american-lower-class-earns.html

[14] Ibid.

[15] Ibid.

life, the options available to you, and the potential pitfalls and challenges you must be aware of.

We begin with the early years from birth through high school. I will walk you through the decision on whether pursuing a post-secondary education is right for you or your children. We will take a realistic view of the approximate cost associated with that additional education and attempt to analyze the cost/benefit of such decisions. Our discussion will cover an undergraduate education, as well as graduate studies.

It is important to note that the costs associated with these decisions will often follow you through the next phase of your financial life as you begin your career. We will discuss how to best prepare yourself for decisions such as geographic considerations, job opportunities, salary and benefit packages, growth potential, expense breakdown, quality of life, life balance considerations, social network considerations, and taxes.

As you age and mature financially, there are many important factors to consider. What are the financial ramifications of a live-in versus a marital relationship? Our planning will help you prepare for transitioning from a one to two-person household. We will explore these considerations in detail, as failure to do so can cause irreparable damage, both emotionally and financially.

As you move on to having children, we take our planning to a whole new level. The expenses of raising a child, depending on geographic location, has been estimated to be approximately $233,610 but may be higher depending on where you live.[16] Note that this is the cost before college expenses are included. We will discuss why a financial analysis should be done *before* such a decision is made.

This book will help you to think "big picture" and factor in the many variables that should be considered when two people (or perhaps a single parent) make such monumental decisions. We will explore all the factors that should be considered from both, a financial, and emotional perspective.

The planning journey continues as you enter the later stages of your working years. There is a myriad of costs to consider as you prepare to enter retirement. We will take a look at all the family costs that should be considered. These are things like post K-12 education considerations, costs of young-adult children, financial obligations to aging parents and grandparents, budget considerations, retirement considerations, health, health care costs, and many others.

---

[16] Tim Parker. "The Cost of Raising a Child in America." *Investopedia.* Updated May 20, 2019. https://www.investopedia.com/articles/personal-finance/090415/cost-raising-child-america.asp

As one enters the end of the accumulation phase of investing, it is time for a "come to Jesus" self-assessment of one's financial, health and future goals/desires. This chapter will likely be the most important part of the book as it will provide a measurement of how well you have done in each of these areas up to this point in time.

Examining the interconnectivity between different aspects of your life is essential in determining decisions regarding how you will live in retirement, continue employment, transition into a semi-retirement, or completely retire from your job. Included in this chapter are some thought-provoking tips that will help you anticipate "what if" situations that could arise throughout your life and prepare you to address them.

Finally, we will briefly discuss the later stages of your life about remaining healthy, relevant, engaged, and financially capable of living within your means. That may be at home, with assistance, with children, or as you move to an exciting, new senior housing development.

We will discuss the reasons why estate planning should be reviewed on a regular basis. I will give you guidance on what family documents you may need such as durable powers of attorney and living trust documents. These are important when making wise decisions regarding health, financial, and end-of-life issues.

What does this have to do with a planning book? Everything.

This book is intended to be a general roadmap for introducing the concepts of planning and to help you avoid my sister, Donna's fate. It is certainly not a one-size-fits-all solution, but it can be a roadmap for the hundreds of thousands of people who want and need direction or face financial challenges.

My goal is to educate you if you desire guidance and to help you recalibrate to a path of success. My hope is that you may find yourself in a much better place than you were yesterday, regardless of what stage you begin your journey. All it takes is a little bit of planning!

CHAPTER 1

Parents and Children: Starting Off Right

What parent doesn't want their child to be responsible, compassionate, and financially literate? If we want to see these attributes and skills grow in our children, it is important that we plant those seeds early and often.

Financial illiteracy in this country is reaching epidemic proportions. Every three years, FINRA, a key financial regulatory agency, conducts a survey of five questions designed to gauge financial literacy in this country. The questions cover key financial topics such as interest rates, inflation, risk, mortgages, stocks, and bonds. Between 2009-2015, Americans got worse at answering these questions.[17]

The U.S. ranks 14th globally in financial literacy, which means we beat Botswana but fall behind developed countries such as Germany and Canada.[18] With only 16.4% of U.S. students required to take a personal finance class in high school, what do we expect?[19]

The areas of responsibility and compassion are equally challenging these days. As people become more and more attached to their electronic devices and less engaged in the real world, it is critical that these qualities are nurtured from a young age.

A recent article in Parenting Magazine offers some valuable insight. "Teaching this (compassion, empathy, responsibility) doesn't mean lectures or visits to soup kitchens. It's part of day-to-day life: how you answer your child's questions, how you solve conflict at the park, how you nudge his or her growing capacity to understand and think about other people."[20]

---

[17] Jeff Desjardins. "America's Growing Financial Literacy Problem." *Visual Capitalist.* October 28, 2018. https://www.visualcapitalist.com/americas-growing-financial-literacy-problem/.
[18] Ibid.
[19] Ibid.
[20] Jane Meredith Adams. "Raising a Compassionate Child." *Parenting.* Accessed March 17, 2020. https://www.parenting.com/child/raising-a-compassionate-child/

Children learn more from our actions than they do almost anything else. If you want your children to be compassionate, show your child and those around you compassion. The same is true for empathy and responsibility. You are your child's first role model. Set a good example and take the time to explain to them *why* you chose to handle a conflict a certain way. Every moment can be a teaching moment.

Volunteering and Community Service

One of the best ways to teach children how to be responsible, empathetic, and compassionate is to involve them in volunteering and community service. Volunteering gives children an opportunity to see how other people live, helping them to build empathy. When kids can think about others' experiences, it gives them new perspective on their own challenges. This can increase their coping skills and significantly impact the way they live their lives.

Volunteering and community service are also great activities to do together as a family. Caring for others helps parents and children develop patience and cultivate deeper relationships. Both qualities are also essential to developing a sense of well-being and happiness. These, in turn, can also be linked to better health and longevity.

Dr. Andrew Steptoe, a psychologist from University College London conducted a five-year study on older individuals age 52-79 to study the link between happiness, health, and longevity. "Older people were up to 35% less likely to die during the five-year study if they reported feeling happy, excited, and content on a typical day."[21] Even more interesting, Dr. Steptoe found that the "absence of happiness" may be even more important to health and longevity than the "presence of negative emotions."[22]

Service is also a great way for kids to learn the value and benefits of teamwork. It gives them many opportunities to discover and develop their own natural leadership skills in addition to helping them nurture critical thinking and problem-solving skills.

And of course, we all know volunteering and community service helps kids get into college and there is

---

[21] Amanda MacMillan. "Happiness Linked to Longer Life." *CNN*. updated July 20, 2018. https://www.cnn.com/2011/10/31/health/happiness-linked-longer-life/index.html

[22] Ibid.

a reason for that. Colleges do everything they can to attract quality people. Empathy has its benefits and rewards when starting to interact with such institutions.

Financial Literacy

Simply put, financial literacy involves the understanding of a variety of financial areas including the basics of personal finance, borrowing, and investing. Current trends show a steady decline in financial literacy in this country.

This is alarming considering now more than ever, people are carrying credit card debt, student loan debt, and mortgage debt, often simultaneously. In addition to that, individuals are also expected to manage their own retirement accounts and invest personal assets online. Financial choices, in general, are becoming more complicated at a time when government assistance is drying up (this of course was prior to the Covidvirus19 era).

When you consider that people are spending almost as much time in retirement as they did in their working years and Social Security was originally designed to last only five to six years, you can see that financial literacy is no longer a luxury but rather, an absolute necessity. It is imperative that individuals understand basic financial principles because they are being asked to shoulder more and more responsibility for investment decisions in their retirement accounts. This directly impacts your future and those around you.

It is so important to begin to teach your children about money at an early age. A child inherits their initial perceptions about money from their situation at home. A family's socio-economic status is directly related to the challenges and opportunities a child may face with their own finances in the future. However, with focused effort, it's still possible for a child to overcome the birth lottery and achieve more financial knowledge and security than their parents.

Almost from birth, a child begins to develop their own behavioral habits. Kids are bombarded with messages about money every day. These include ads, peer pressure to spend, societal influences that encourage spending, and, of course, parental modeling. Your goal as a parent is to model strong positive thoughts, feelings, and behaviors around money that can counteract the power of social and marketing influences.

Chances are your child will not receive any significant financial literacy education at school. Your child's financial education and literacy falls to you and every day is a classroom. Play money games with your children. There are many from which to choose. Dave Ramsey offers games and tools geared specifically to children. It's also important to talk to your children about money. In a recent study conducted by Money Confident Kids, only 23% of the kids surveyed said that they talk to their parents about money on a regular basis.[23]

Financial literacy is one of the most important lessons you can ever teach your children. For better or worse, money will become a growing focus as they go through life. You cannot depend on the schools to teach them what they need to know about money. As more and more of the financial responsibility of retirement is shifted to the individual, it's critical that your child has a strong financial foundation.

---

[23] "A Primer for Financial Literacy for Kids." *National Financial Educator's Council.* Accessed March 20, 2020. https://www.financialeducatorscouncil.org/financial-literacy-for-kids/

Technology

The concepts of financial literacy, volunteerism, and responsibility are obviously important concepts for both parents and children to grasp and appreciate. However, these important life lessons can also help to build a shared connection between parents and children.

As kids become increasingly more plugged into technology and their devices, they often become more disengaged and distant. Because of this, finding new ways to build bridges of connection between parents and children has taken on a new sense of urgency.

On average, U.S. teens spend more than 7 hours per day on their screens.[24] Even tweens spend almost 5 hours each day on non-school-related screen time. In fact, average screen time has increased 42 minutes per day since 2015.[25]

This screen obsession is not an isolated problem in the US. It captured international attention when South Korea's Ministry of Gender Equality and Family created

---

[24] Kristen Rogers. "U.S Teens Use Screens More Than Seven Hours a Day On Average—And That's Not Including School Work." *CNN.* October 29, 2019. https://www.cnn.com/2019/10/29/health/common-sense-kids-media-use-report-wellness/index.html

[25] Ibid.

16 detox camps across the country, where parents enrolled their children to try to break them of their technology addiction.

When analyzed further, this issue was thought to stem from the heavy academic load the country places on its youth. This results in little time left for relaxation or a proper work/life balance. In fact, according to the 2015 study, only around 46% of 15-year-olds in South Korea engage in any sort of exercise or athletics.[26] This is the lowest of any of the 36 countries participating in the Organization for Cooperation and Development, established in 1961.[27]

It is important that parents develop a working understanding with solid communication and an accountability system when dealing with children, technology, and social media. Connecting with kids and setting boundaries when it comes to technology and their devices can quickly become an emotionally charged issue, especially when dealing with teens.

Technology consumes an ever-increasing portion of most kids' days, often at the expense of proper nutrition, exercise, and participation in community and extracurricular activities. Poor habits if not addressed

---

[26] Ibid.

[27] Ibid.

can carry over to other parts of their lives. Not only are these activities critical to good health, but as kids continue to withdraw into their electronic devices, these activities take on a new social relevance.

Exercise and participation in sports or other school and community activities teaches kids self-discipline and gives them an opportunity to establish real friendships. It can also teach them valuable business skills such as teamwork and networking. These kinds of life skills are far more difficult to grasp in a purely electronic environment.

It Takes a Village

Community collaboration and involvement can help to play a key role in getting kids the foundation they need in these areas, but especially in financial literacy. Sheila Miller's Financial Smarts for Students is a perfect example of what a huge difference these programs can make in the lives of children.

Sheila has taught high school business classes for twenty-five years in Newfoundland High School in New Hampshire. In 2001, she recognized that her students lacked the financial knowledge necessary to function in today's world. Sheila took the initiative to introduce a financial literacy program into her small, rural high school and she found that students were immediately drawn to the subject matter.

In 2007-2008, she took a leadership role in bringing the Jumpstart Financial Smarts for Students program to her school. Her timing could not have been more perfect, as the Great Recession of 2008 was just beginning. Today, Newfoundland High School is one of only eight New Hampshire high schools that require students to take both an Economics class and a standalone Personal Finance class.

Based on the annual 2017 NH Jumpstart Coalition report, New Hampshire high schools have made little progress in preparing students to be financially literate as they make their way in the world. As of 2017, the following was reported:

- 12% of NH high schools require a standalone course in Personal Finance for graduation.[28]

- 62% of NH high schools offer Personal Finance as an elective in addition to meeting

[28] "Survey of New Hampshire High Schools." *JumpStart Financial Smarts For Students*. New Hampshire Coalition 2017.

state requirements for Economics (there seems to be a greater emphasis on getting a kid to understand supply and demand than on understanding how to calculate their take home pay after taxes).[29]

- 14% of NH high schools require Economics only.[30]

Sheila had some interesting insights into the challenges kids face today compared to a decade earlier. She found that kids are so tech savvy these days, it can be difficult for them to comprehend the importance of simple financial basics such as balancing a checkbook. Everything they do is with an app, but Sheila believed students benefit in their teenage years when financial literacy is a requirement in school. Afterall, financial literacy is definitely a requirement in life.

If you have any lasting doubt that this is only a New Hampshire or U.S. problem, think again. Overseas, our major economic competitor China, is itself building a society of poor fiscal consumerism without fully comprehending the consequences. Continual massive growth has come at the hands of not only government spending, but it is resulted in the building of a middle

[29] Ibid.
[30] Ibid.

class of consumers. These people have experienced wage gains over the last couple decades but have failed in financial literacy for its youth.

Regardless of where you live on the globe, easy credit is a death song to those who have little financial acumen. Online lenders such as Ant Financial Services Group have conducted surveys showing that more than 50% of its loans are to people under 30 years of age. This figure may not sound alarming to the party until you understand that Ant charges a 16% annual interest rate on these loans.[31] Surveys further concluded that approximately one-third of these borrowers need this short-term money to repay their other debts.[32] The final nail in the financial literacy coffin is that nearly half of them have missed payments![33]

In the U.S., there are all kinds of resources available to community educators, as well as parents, who wish to work directly with children on a variety of STEM-related subjects including financial literacy education. Some excellent sites you may want to check out:

---

[31] Stella Yifan Xie, Shandi Li and Julie Wernau. "Young Chinese Spend Like Americans and Take on Worrisome Debt." *Wall Street Journal.* August 29, 2019. https://www.wsj.com/articles/young-chinese-spend-like-americansand-take-on-worrisome-debt-11567093953

[32] Ibid.

[33] Ibid.

www.teachbanzai.com

Free online financial literacy program with different banzai levels for each age range.

www.khanacademy.org

Widely recognized online education program.

www.moneyintructor.com

Resources for teaching money skills, personal finances, business, and financial life skills.

www.bizkids.com

Business resources, videos, and lesson plans for teaching kids about personal finance.

www.NGPF.org Next Gen Personal Finance

Free resources for educators or homeschoolers who want to teach a personal finance class.

www.feedthepig.org

Fun tools to help you feed your piggy bank.

www.financialentertainment.org

Offers a wide variety of games and videos for getting young children involved with math and finance.

Another noteworthy collaboration that has helped to sow the seeds of financial literacy in the state of New Hampshire involves Jackie Eastwood, former CEO of Salient Technologies. Jackie knows a thing or two about financial literacy. She founded her company in 1999 and subsequently sold it to Medtronic Inc. in 2011 for $525 Million.

Jackie did not follow the typical path to success. She attended one year of college, before becoming pregnant, getting married, and eventually divorced. She raised her daughter while working at a variety of jobs to support her as a single parent. After several years as a waitress, she entered the sales industry and worked her way up the ladder at Medtronic.

After retiring from the company, she decided to form another company based off the purchase of a Medtronic device that had been shelved and never brought into production. This company was TissueLink, Inc. A/K/A Salient Technologies. To this day, Jackie remains very active not only in her educational pursuits but also in business around the state.

Currently, as a Trustee for the University System of New Hampshire, Jackie believes that the present curriculum in schools does not provide children with enough skills to address ever-changing workforce needs, especially in the areas of business and financial literacy. She has become a fierce advocate for alternative learning options such as VLACS (Virtual Learning Academy Charter School). This is a self-paced institution in Exeter, NH. It provides both a physical facility and online access to more than 10,000 students from brick-and-mortar schools throughout New Hampshire.

While virtual schools have experienced their share of controversary and poor results, VLACS is a success story. In 2016, full-time students modestly exceeded New Hampshire's average scores on state reading and math tests. They also beat New Hampshire's average SAT scores. Regardless of whether students utilize VLACS on a full-time basis or as a needed supplement for filling in educational gaps they may be experiencing, the institution is a valuable tool to New Hampshire youth.

I know from personal experience how important it is to guide your children in their early and teenage years. While most parents may believe they know best, it is important to remain flexible enough to let them find their own way as they grow and mature.

My son Grant was the starting catcher at Exeter High School and had been involved in athletics at a very early age. In his sophomore year, he expressed a desire to suddenly quit high school baseball. While initially disappointed that my dream of being the parent of a future Red Sox Hall of Fame catcher had evaporated, I respected his decision. I did, however, inform him that if he chose not to participate in high school athletics, he had to get a job. After much discussion, he applied for and was accepted as a paid intern with Global Relief Technologies, Inc., a boutique engineering, and technology firm. Although the firm had previously awarded paid internships only to those studying engineering in college, Grant's strong background in math and desire to learn convinced the company's CEO to bring him on board.

From his sophomore through senior years, Grant worked an average of ten hours per week for the firm. He was even nominated for a six-week summer program at Cal Tech. Although he was not selected to participate in the program, he flew out to California and went through the entire interview process, which was a great experience for him.

He went on to graduate from a five-year Chemical Engineering program at Northeastern University. Although I am a strong believer in high school athletics, I believe the entire intern experience better equipped my son to finish a challenging educational program and function more effectively in the real world.

This is a perfect example of why it is so important to provide children with structure while always remaining open and flexible. One digital tool for assisting in establishing financial structure is Greenlight, an online banking resource. You can learn more at greenlightcard.com. They provide a spending account for customers with parental controls. It is like your child having a debit card that you control not only where, but how much they can spend.

With a $4.99/month subscription, your child can open a savings account that you (the parent) set up and pay interest on. You can help your child set goals and track their progress. You can even monitor your child's weekly chores and pay. All of this requires minimal setup and the benefits of implementing this foundational process are huge.

Planting the seeds of financial literacy from an early age helps children mature in their understanding of costs and debt. Both are extremely important when considering college—a subject covered extensively in the next chapter.

Chapter 1 Action Steps

1. Engage in family-related activities that will help children develop a foundation for better understanding the value and concept of money. These can include volunteerism and charitable inclinations. You want your children to appreciate that giving time and/or money can feel good! Do it as a family and create a new dynamic that is very different from athletic-oriented activities.

2. Utilize online education sites that are both fun and educational for children.

3. Focus school activities that are include a balance of athletic and education areas.

4. Introduce children to people that can be potential mentors as the child ages.

5. Inspire children to intern in their teenage years and explore activities that may generate a passion for a particular career. Additionally, work

with them so they understand how this work now could translate into future financial opportunities.

6. Become very involved in helping children align these interests with potential post K-12 education.

CHAPTER 2

A Family's College Cost/Benefit Analysis

Everyone knows that college is one of the largest costs incurred in raising a child. It is a huge, expensive decision, and one that should be reached only after an extensive and in-depth analysis by the child, the parents, and a guidance counselor.

Many different variables must be examined when choosing whether college is the best option and if so, the best college for your child. Some variables you will definitely want to consider:

- Assessment of the student's educational level
- Grades, effort, course study, extracurricular activities
- Maturity level
- Self-discipline, leadership, community involvement
- Affordability and proximity of college to home
- Realistic assessment of the student regarding peer pressure
    - ➢ This may indicate the appropriateness of joining or not joining fraternities or sororities

Parents and children should work together to complete the FAFSA. This is a free application completed by current and incoming college students in the U.S. to determine student financial aid eligibility. Also, students should work with parents and guidance counselors to determine what scholarships may be available and get those applications completed by their appropriate deadlines.

Regardless of whether your child's scholarship applications were successful, it is still a valuable learning experience for them. They begin to gain an appreciation for the value of an education versus its costs and may even begin to appreciate you more!

If your child is not ready or able to afford college upon high school graduation, you may want to consider temporary or permanent financial arrangements. It's important to discuss these alternatives as a family. Areas you may want to consider are:

- Will the child be living at home or on their own?
- Will the student be financially subsidized by the parents? And if so, what does that look like?
- Always discuss expectations
    - You and your child's
    - Temporary vs. permanent

College is a huge expense, so you want to do everything in your power to ensure a wise decision the first time. I recently met a wonderful woman while traveling in the Greek Islands and the Amalfi Coast of Italy. Dana Ferniany is one of the most gracious people you could ever meet on a cruise. She was on the trip, not for her own benefit, but rather to accompany a dear friend, whose bucket list included an international cruise over to Greece and Italy.

Dana was from Birmingham, Alabama, and grew up in a family with little means but lots of love. Her father worked at Russell Athletic Mills where he invented the "tear-away jersey," (for all you football fans) and was eventually inducted into the Sporting Goods Hall of Fame.

Dana worked hard to earn her teaching degree. She eventually got married and had three wonderful children. Even with children, she continued teaching gifted students for more than twenty years.

In 1992, her husband, Will had an opportunity to oversee the marketing department for the University of Pennsylvania Health Systems. After leaving her home state of Alabama, Dana decided to spend the next chapter of her life focused on exploring all that the Philadelphia region had to offer. She went back to college and eventually over the years obtained three master's degrees in varying areas of study.

Dana acknowledges very few regrets in life. She attends church, is a strong, caring woman and by all accounts has a wonderful forty-year (and counting) marriage. When I asked her if she and her husband wished they had done anything differently, she mentioned that her children now have doctoral degrees in Veterinary Medicine and Education, respectively. However, that was only after they each obtained undergraduate degrees that had nothing to do with their current careers.

Dana said that in hindsight, she wished that she and her husband had worked closer with their children on goals and planning prior to their college entrance. She wished they would have vetted their children's passions better and given them some time, rather than pushing them to move immediately into college life without clarity on a career path.

Although her kids eventually found their calling, her children spent additional time and Dana incurred unnecessary expenses in the process. While it could very well be, that their initial detour provided some eventual guidance in leading them to their current careers, it does make for an expensive, time-consuming experimental process.

While everything worked out well for Dana and her kids, many other people are not as lucky. Limited finances can significantly impact your ability to hit the redo button when aligning education with the working career you were meant to pursue.

My son Adam's story further reinforces Dana's. Every child is different, and Adam just did not apply himself in his K-12 years. Whether it was laziness, lack of maturity, ADD, or a combination of these, he learned a valuable life lesson: everything has a price. The price he paid for failing to put in the time or effort in high school was his parent's refusal to pay for him to attend a four-year college. This prevented him from staying on the same educational timeline as his classmates as they moved onto a post–K-12 college.

Initially, such action wounded our son's pride and feelings of self-worth. While many might have had feelings of resentment or fallen into permanent despair, Adam never gave up. As the weeks, months, and years passed, he matured and decided to enroll in a local community college for two years before moving on to Southern NH University to complete his four-year degree. He graduated with Cum Laude honors and now works at Bain Company in IT. Adam's story demonstrates just how important it is for kids to have parental guidance as they navigate this tricky and expensive phase of their lives. His story may have ended quite differently without it.

If college is the right choice for your child, it is important that both of you are confident that the field of study is an employable one. Equally important to discuss with your child is their motivation for that choice. Do they have a natural passion for their field, or do they want to pursue it for some alternative reason such as money or status?

As of 2019, the following careers are ranked as to the highest paying, those with the lowest stress levels and a combination of the two.

Highest Paying Careers of 2019

1. Physician. Median Base Salary: $193,415
2. Pharmacy Manager. Median Base Salary: $144,768
3. Dentist. Median Base Salary: $142,478
4. Pharmacist. Median Base Salary: $126,438
5. Enterprise Architect. Median Base Salary: $122,585
6. Corporate Counsel. Median Base Salary: $117,588
7. Software Engineering Manager. Median Base Salary: $114,163

8. Physician Assistant. Median Base Salary: $113,855
9. Corporate Controller. Median Base Salary: $113,368
10. Software Development Manager. Median Base Salary: $109,80[34]

Lowest Stress Careers of 2019

1. Diagnostic Medical Sonographer. Median Salary: $71, 410
2. Compliance Officer. Median Salary: $67,870
3. Hair Stylist. Median Salary: $25,850
4. Audiologist. Median Salary: $75,820
5. University Professor. Median Salary: $76,000
6. Medical Records Technician. Median Salary: $39,180
7. Jeweler. Median Salary: $37,960
8. Operations Research Analyst. Median Salary: $81,390

[34]Emily Moore. "Highest Paid Careers of 2019." Posted on September 17, 2019. https://www.glassdoor.com/blog/highest-paying-jobs-2019/

9. Pharmacy Technician. Median Salary: $31,750
10. Massage Therapist. Median Salary: $39,990[35]

Highest-Paying, Low-Stress Jobs in the U.S.

1. Orthodontist. Median Salary $208,000
2. Statistician. Median Salary $84,060
3. Radiation Therapist. Median Salary $80,570
4. Web Developer. Median Salary $67,990
5. Cartographer. Median Salary $63,990
6. Anthropologist. Median Salary $62,280
7. Archaeologist. Median Salary $62,280
8. Hearing Aid Specialist. Median Salary $54,860
9. Survey Researcher. Median Salary $54,270
10. Wind Turbine Technician. Median Salary $53,880[36]

---

[35] "2019 Least Stressful Jobs." Accessed November 30, 2019. https://www.careercast.com/jobs-rated/least-stressful-2019?page=9/

[36] Jennifer Liu. "The Highest-Paying, Low-Stress Job in The U.S. Pays $208,000 a Year." *CNBC.* October 2, 2019. https://www.cnbc.com/2019/10/01/us-news-world-report-10-highest-paying-lowest-stress-jobs.html

During their time in college, students should begin adding work experience to their educational experience as soon as possible. Obviously, positions that offer an opportunity to work in their field or a field related to their own is optimal. These could include programs like internships, work in the community, aide positions, or co-ops. As you are researching colleges, it's a good idea to also gauge the level of commitment each university you're considering has to these kinds of programs.

Another wise move as a parent is to discuss what portion of your student's college earnings will be saved versus spent for living expenses. At this juncture, it makes sense to carve out a few hours to work with your child on putting together a preliminary budget. Have this conversation before your student has even landed their first college job. If you discuss this early, it will not come as a shock to your child. Afterall, it's a foundational lesson in —pay yourself first and understand how you are spending the set amount of remaining dollars you have at your disposal.

There are many components to a comprehensive college planning analysis. Of course, financial considerations are primary but there are many intangibles that can also have a significant impact on your decisions and the entire college experience. Give yourself adequate time to make a quality decision. Make those decisions with your child and do not hesitate to call in other professionals to ensure you're making the best college decisions possible for your child and your family.

Chapter 2 Action Plan

1. Take a survey or work with an advisor to assess both you and your child's situation before making any decisions regarding college. Your goals should be to gain more clarity on: the readiness of your child, their goals and aspirations, their maturity level relative to the opportunity, affordability, determining how to pay (parent, child, combination), and geographic considerations (close to home or far away).

2. Talk with school advisors to discuss career choices and how they line up with your child's background. Do they make sense or not? If not, delaying college in lieu of personal discovery time may make the most sense for your child. For instance, if your child never liked or did well in math and suddenly decides he wants to become an accountant, actuarial, or statistician, that should raise a red flag. A better option may be to take significantly less expensive

community college math courses and see how they do.

3. Balance college education with work related activities (internships, co-ops, etc.) to better align learning with real life opportunities. Continue to explore career opportunities, geographic locations, and compensation ranges during this time.

4. Enjoy the college experience responsibly. There may be times when you may be the only adult in the room during non-school social times.

5. Download and complete an interactive budget at: **jaylevyplanning.net** or email at **jaylevyplanning@gmail.com**

CHAPTER 3

Adult Life Gets More Complicated

Funding a college education is no doubt a substantial expense that requires careful thought and evaluation. However, that is the easy part. Life begins to get more complicated once the diploma is in hand and it is time to start a real career.

Landing that first professional job after college is a major milestone for every graduate. Unfortunately, all too often I see them focus almost exclusively on salary. While this is obviously an important piece of the puzzle, there are many other factors to consider when trying to decide on that first monumental career choice.

This chapter is dedicated to your graduate. In it, it covers factors to consider when giving them a firm foundation and getting them off to a good start in life. Hopefully over the years, you have planted strategic seeds of wisdom in your child that have taken root, and you're starting to see this blossom as they begin their adult life.

Although your job as a parent may be winding down a bit, your child still needs your wisdom and guidance—whether they realize it or not. While it is imperative that they make their own decisions, continue to remind them that you are always available as a sounding board they can utilize for all major decisions in life. This includes both an analytical and emotional perspectives. As the years go by, they will come to cherish this support more than you can imagine.

If your child is more analytical, provide them with an emotional perspective to balance their left- brain dominance. If they are more emotional by nature, begin to teach them how to approach decisions and challenges from an analytical basis. Both components are integral to good decision-making.

Every child is different with different opportunities and preferences. The following are some variables you and your graduate may want to consider when making those first career decisions fresh out of college. Please note that for the balance of this chapter, I will be talking directly to your graduate.

Geography

Believe it or not, geographic considerations begin with a very honest, internal analysis of self and your emotional makeup. This includes an accurate assessment of your strengths and limitations. Most people are aware of their strengths. Your own limitations may not always be as easy to recognize but are still important to know. Identifying your limits is not an exercise designed to make you feel bad about yourself. We all have limits and it is important to know yours, so your decisions are wise and rooted.

Are you more comfortable being close to family, friends, and your regular support group? Or are you ready to get as far away from your hometown as possible? Out with the old and in with the new! Neither is right or wrong. In fact, most people fall somewhere on the continuum rather than at one extreme or the other. You must determine what is right for you at this juncture in your life.

If you grew up in a small town and went to a local university, you may feel more comfortable sticking closer to home right out of college. Moving thousands of miles away to a major metropolitan area to start your new life may sound exciting. However, even if the initial job opportunity has potential and pays well, moving away from a strong support system may cause undue stress and anxiety that could have been avoided.

This is when it pays to brutally honest with yourself. It is important that you do not allow the novelty and excitement of a new adventure to overshadow a more realistic view of what life would look like outside of your comfort zone and far from friends and family.

On the other hand, you may have developed a good social network during your college years. You may be familiar with certain companies in a co-op or perhaps you worked as an intern for a specific company while in college. When you are already familiar with a company or have an established social network within the company or in the area, the anxiety associated with such a monumental move will likely be far less.

For more clarity, an exercise I frequently recommend to clients involves creating your own personalized questionnaire. Develop questions that require both positive and negative analysis.

For example:

- What are the benefits of moving to a new geographic location?
- What would be the primary challenges or negatives to moving to a new geographic location?
- Assign a numeric value to each benefit and challenge based on their importance to you.

Answer as completely and comprehensively as you can. You will find as you answer the questions above, it will lead into some of the other key areas that we will cover later in this chapter.

Say for instance, you have determined that taking a position away from family or a significant other is a "negative." Your next step would be to analyze the job, the compensation, and do a budget analysis to see to what degree these factors offset the perceived "negative" of moving away. If you decide the position is a viable option, your next step may be to price plane tickets back home so you have a rough idea of how often you can fly in to visit.

Ideally, your questionnaire should include life-balance questions we do not always think about. While proximity to hospitals or medical facilities may not seem like an issue to a healthy young person, it is very important if you suffer from diabetes or have chronic health issues.

Another example of life-balance issues you do not want to overlook concerns leisure activities. If you can't wait for the first snow to hit the ski slopes, you may want to consider how happy you would be taking a job in Florida or Nebraska, where a slope may be defined as a steep driveway in Lincoln! Consider what other life-balance issues might be important to you. Be sure to include questions covering each of these areas.

Do not hesitate to call on your support system to help you with your decision. Compare the process to establishing your own personal board of directors. Family, friends, and other close advisors you have met through the years are great resources to utilize. Their role is to provide you with different perspectives as well as guidance as you begin to establish a structured decision-making process.

Also, as part of your personal dossier, keep your self-assessment questionnaire in your permanent files. You can gain valuable perspective from a periodic review. It gives you clarity on what your priorities were previously and how they may have changed.

Finally, when faced with additional career moves, revisit these questions and completely new assessments. I have found this process worth its weight in gold to young people as they begin their adult life.

Job Opportunity

There is more to consider when analyzing potential job opportunities than strictly compensation. It is important to look at the complete employment package offered. This includes not only compensation but also considers the overall benefits package, as well as intangibles that are important to you personally.

When conducting an overall benefits analysis, there are several areas you will want to examine. You will want to carefully review the medical insurance offered—your cost and the portion the company pays. You will also want to look at the company retirement plan and what kind of match they offer. What kind of disability and life insurance is offered? Will you be eligible for any kind of bonus, and if so, on what criteria is it based? Finally, become familiar with the company stock options program if one is offered.

This is a time when reaching out to your personal board of directors (BOD) is of great value. However, this decision will require deeper introspection on your part. One of the first things you will want to determine is how well the job opportunity aligns with your passions or your field of study. Another productive method of viewing an employment opportunity is to examine the future potential of the job. Analyze what opportunities the position could lead to in one, five, or ten years.

You will likely want to develop a second personal questionnaire that includes questions such as:

- What are the benefits of accepting this job offer?
- What are the negatives of accepting it?
- How many hours will you be working?
- Do increased hours and compensation justify a compromise in life-balance issues?
- How does accepting this offer align with your passions and desires?

The last question is a good indication of how well your education aligns with the job choice you are considering. If you received a BA in Accounting, you would likely feel far more comfortable pursuing a management position at a bank compared to someone with an engineering degree taking a position in retail sales.

Using your personal questionnaire self-analysis will give you a tool for evaluating various issues that tend to overwhelm young people, especially at this early state of your adult life. I remember my son Grant was extremely gifted in math. In fact, his Stratham, NH, Math Counts Club won the state championship during two of his three years during junior high school. He knew much more than I did on the subject, and he repeatedly reminded me of this throughout his teenage years.

Begrudgingly, years later, and even with his aptitude for math, he had to put in a call to his mother to discuss his first Massachusetts W2. On the condition that I would not lecture him, my wife, Kelly, brokered a phone conversation between the two of us so I could bring him up to speed regarding FICA and state income taxes. To say that he was not a happy camper would be an understatement!

To gauge how the salary, you are being offered measures up, you will want to pull some income comparisons for the particular industry and job description you are considering. Be sure to also include an evaluation of the benefits package being offered relative to the geographic location you are considering. While salary will be the major component of any employment package, it's important to also quantify the other benefits being offered such as paid vacation and personal days, medical, disability and life insurance provided, bonus opportunities, and stock option programs.

There are numerous sites which provide data that you can either assess yourself online, through your college advisor, or through staff employment agencies or headhunters. It is wise to remember that depending on the industry and stage of company's existence, you may need to look past initial starting salary to truly assess the potential of the position.

A start-up technology firm will tend not to be as competitive as one that has been around long enough to show a history of consistent revenue and profitability. To compensate for a shortfall in salary, they may offer incentives such as ownership through a stock option program that could be quite lucrative in the future. This is a perfect situation in which to call on your personal board of directors to help you understand and offer guidance during the consideration process.

You will also want to prepare yourself for all the various tax and benefit costs that will inevitably reduce your paycheck. Social Security, disability, Medicare, federal and state income taxes (if applicable), along with a variety of deductions associated with deferred or after-tax contributions to retirement accounts, health insurance, disability, life, or other insurance. All of this will chip away at what you eventually bring home. Do not be surprised if you see your salary, which started as a giant redwood tree get reduced to a pine, maple, and in some cases, even a shrub after taxes and benefit costs are deducted.

Finally, one should consider intangibles associated with the company and position you may agree to take.

- Is traveling involved, and if so, how much?
- Do you consider travel a positive or a negative?
- Does the company offer paid educational opportunities either through job-related certifications, training, or other graduate programs?
- Depending on your specific field of study, this may be a tremendous value that you cannot quantify with initial salary projections.

Budgeting

This is where your choice to skip those college finance courses may come back to haunt you. The good news is that you can utilize online resources for a crash course in budgeting. Although it is not rocket science, you will want to develop a basic process for setting up your budgeting spreadsheet. It should list your "fixed" and your "discretionary" expenses as well as what you are left with in your net take-home pay. It is simple to do but not necessarily a fun or enjoyable experience.

In one of my favorite books of all time, *Dollars and Sense*, the authors offer valuable insight into the average person's behavioral relationship with money. It's interesting to note that people tend to behave very differently when paying cash (it's very painful and impacts behavior more conservatively) versus paying by credit card (no immediate pain and may feel the purchase is almost free at the purchase point) versus paying by debit card (which lies somewhere between the other two).

When I was serving as the NH Financial Chairman for Governor Tim Pawlenty's presidential bid in 2010, there was a common theme in his speeches that I found very interesting. He used to say that people will behave very differently at a wedding reception based on if the bar is “cash” or “open”.

Establishing an actual budget tends to go against the very grain of our society in the 21st century. The ease and creation of financial tools have made promoting consumerism easier with each passing year. Think about it. For every community message about overextending oneself with debt, there are two or three “what’s in your wallet” jingles. Based on the record high levels of debt with credit cards, student education, auto loans, corporate, individual states, and the federal government, essentially, there are not a lot of “grown-ups” when it comes to finances.

Personal budgeting can be painful. Sticking with the budget you do establish can be even more painful—but well worth the effort. Remember, my goal in this book is to give you the information and tools you need to separate yourself from the masses.

Take the time to categorize each expense you know you will have each month. This is called a “fixed” expense. Rent or mortgage, transportation, food, utilities, insurance, student loans, credit card loans (could be from a combination of fixed and discretionary spending) all fall under the fixed cost label. “Discretionary” expenses are those expenses that you have control over, and these can vary each month. This would include things like clothing, entertainment, eating out, vacations, etc.

Financial writer, Michael Kitces suggests taking the "discretionary" aspect of the budget one step further by developing a discretionary sub-classification. He recommends allocating the percentage of discretionary income you need to feel emotionally satisfied (for fun), while earmarking the remaining percentage to saving, building an emergency fund, or making additional contributions to your retirement accounts (in essence transferring back into "fixed expenses").

No discussion on budgeting is complete without addressing the "D" word: debt. It is important to get a handle on how much is owed on individual loans, interest rates being charged for each obligation, and what your minimum monthly required payment is on each. After your minimum payments are budgeted, make some sort of additional payment, even if it is minimal on your highest interest obligations.

Remember that your additional payments will come at the expense of your other discretionary spending. It is important to not only budget but also consider your income and the other assets that you own. If applicable, consider refinancing or consolidation options that could bring your overall interest rate down. Always keep an eye on your credit score to be sure such courses of action won't affect it.

Be aware of potential scams associated with debt-relief services, especially as it relates to student loans. Student debt has been soaring with nearly $1.5 trillion now supplementing credit card debt as the highest debt obligations by consumers. In addition, according to the NY Federal Reserve, a record $89.2 billion was in default with that number likely worsening with an estimated 11% or $160 billion classified as at least 90 days past due.[37]

There are a number of companies that have reportedly been accused of scamming students seeking consolidation guidance services for excessive fees, masquerading as being government-approved and falsifying paperwork submitted to the government (unbeknownst to student) to apply for debt relief. In summary, steer clear of consolidation services and develop your own system for dealing with debt. All it takes is a little foresight and diligence.

---

[37] Jean Eaglesham, Michael Tobin, Coulte Jones. "Soaring Student Debt Opens Door To Relief Scams." *Wall Street Journal.* August 26, 2019. https://www.wsj.com/articles/soaring-student-debt-opens-door-to-relief-scams-11566826805

Renting or Owning

Unfortunately for Millennials and Generation Z, the days of following in their parents' financial footsteps are over. Because of decades of wage inflation that has not kept pace with the cost of home ownership, most young people are unable to graduate from college, get a job, and in a few years buy a home.

It is even more difficult if you are looking for a place that is located in an area experiencing a local economic boom. The city of Seattle is a perfect example. Back in 1989, the median price of a home was $77,300 or $167,773 in today's dollars.[38] Today the median price is a whopping $542,700.[39]

In other words, even if you can afford to put 20% down or $108,540 you would face a monthly mortgage, with insurance and real estate taxes in the vicinity of $2,500/month. To get past the first of two house-qualifying ratios, you'd need a starting gross income of around $90,000 per year and that's just the

---

[38] Julia Carpenter. "Your Parents' Financial Advice is (Kind Of) Wrong." *Wall Street Journal.* September 13, 2019. https://www.wsj.com/articles/your-parents-financial-advice-is-kind-of-wrong-11568367000

[39] Ibid.

first income test.[40] I'm sure that "big gulp" I hear is probably not from a 32oz soda!

The point is, that there is both good and bad news. The good news is that home prices have enjoyed a significant rebound from the Great Recession of 2008. "After falling 33% during the recession, housing prices have returned to peak levels, growing 51% since hitting the bottom of the market. The average house price is now 1% higher than it was at the peak in 2006."[41]

The bad news for people leaving school to start their working careers is that prices have enjoyed a significant rebound from 2008! With lending practices more conservative and wage inflation significantly below housing inflation, it has become increasingly difficult for recent graduates—especially those with significant student debt—to afford the required down payments necessary to become a new homeowner.

A company, HSH.com, tracks mortgage rates around the country. Among HSH's reports are quarterly estimates of the annual income needed to qualify for a median mortgage in the 50 largest metro areas in the U. S. If you do not live in one of those areas, do not fret.

---

[40] Ibid.

[41] "Evaluating the Housing Market Since the Great Recession." Accessed December 26, 2019. https://www.corelogic.com/downloadable-docs/corelogic-peak-totrough-final-030118.pdf.

The purpose is to give you an idea if your place of considered residence is above or below the median.

It also assumes a 20% down, 30-year fix rate mortgage with a standard 28% debt-to-income ratio for buyers. To give a "big picture" view, nationally at the end of the second quarter for 2019 the national median price of a home was $279,600 and that required an annual salary of approximately $61,123.[42] The current end of second quarter interest rates equated to a monthly principle and interest payment of $1426.21.[43]

Remember that this was the national median figure. Here are the numbers on the ten most expensive areas around the country:

#10 Portland Oregon – ASR $83,522, MHP $415,300 which equates to monthly P&I $1,948.85.[44]

#9 Denver, CO – ASR $90,389, MHP $471,400 which equates to monthly P&I $2,109.08.[45]

#8 Washington D.C ASR $94,448, MHP $456,500, which equates to monthly P&I $2203.79

---

[42] Alicia Adamczyk. "The Salary You Need To Buy a Home in 10 of The Largest Cities in The U.S." *CNBC.* October 10, 2019. https://www.cnbc.com/2019/10/10/the-salary-you-need-to-buy-a-house-in-large-us-cities.html.

[43] Ibid.

[44] Ibid.

[45] Ibid.

#7 New York City – ASR $102,237, MHP $420,800 which equates to monthly P&I $2,385.54.[46]

#6 Seattle -ASR $106,618, MHP $542,700, which equates to monthly P&I $2,487.77.[47]

#5 Boston -ASR $107,379, MHP $506,700, which equates to monthly P&I $2,505.53.[48]

#4 Los Angeles – ASR $111,749, MHP $567,000, which equates to monthly P&I $2,607.49.[49]

#3 San Diego – ASR $127,293, MHP $655,00 which equates to monthly P&I of $2970

#2 San Francisco – ASR $201,430, MHP $1,050,000, which equates to monthly P&I $4,700.05.[50]

#1 San Jose – ASR $249,885, MHP $1,330,000, which equates to monthly P&I of $5,831.[51]

Again, this list reflects the top ten most expensive areas, but you can always research to find information that reflects a closer proximity to where you may be looking.[52]

---

[46] Ibid.
[47] Ibid.
[48] Ibid.
[49] Ibid.
[50] Ibid.
[51] Ibid.
[52] Ibid.

When it comes to the ASR (average salary required) of other ranked metro locations, northern areas such as Minneapolis (ASR $63,742) or Milwaukee (ASR $62,997) and southern areas such as Dallas (ASR $65,344) or Raleigh (ASR $60,276) offer more moderate priced options.[53] Regardless, remember this annual salary requirement is just to cover the debt/income ratio for monthly principle and interest after a 20% down payment and a 30-year fixed loan. Other housing costs such as property taxes, insurance, utilities, and maintenance are not included in ASR figures.

Because of this, it should come as no surprise that renting is becoming the most viable option for many young people today. In fact, according to *Reuters,* in December of 2018, "U.S. homebuilding rebounded, driven by a surge in multi-family housing projects, but construction of single-family homes fell to a 1 and 1/2-year low..."[54] This should come as no surprise when you consider that land is becoming a scarcer commodity and more expensive, especially in heavily populated urban areas.

---

[53] Ibid.

[54] Lucia Muntikani. "U.S. Housing Starts Rise, single-family segment still weak." *Reuters*. December 18, 2018. https://www.reuters.com/article/us-usa-economy/u-s-housing-starts-rise-single-family-segment-remains-ewak-idUSKBN1OH1H8

Due to this growing issue, certain states are trying to address this problem by relaxing zoning regulations. One example is Oregon, which, in June of 2019, passed legislation to require cities with populations of more than 25,000 people to allow multi-family dwellings consisting of two to four units to be to be intermingled in areas of single-family homes.[55] The goal of such action is to ultimately create more homes at lower prices.

While there are many who oppose such directives due to the potential for increased traffic, vertical construction constricting sunlight, and the potential social issues from increases in populations (crime, overcrowding of schools, and the potential negative impact on property values), Oregon's efforts are at least making an attempt to address the affordable housing issues that have plagued so many areas of the country. However, short of having a financial source like family subsidizing a home purchase down payment, renting will continue to be the de facto housing arrangement for the foreseeable future.

---

[55] Jeff Mapes. "Oregon Strikes Exclusive Single-Family Zoning But Effects May Take Years." July 3, 2019. https://opb.org/news/article/oregon-single-family-zoning-law-effect-developers/

General Well-Being

One of the most important questions to ask yourself as you transition into your professional life is whether you will feel comfortable, safe, and secure where you may decide to live. This is especially important if your initial job is in a heavily populated city or in an isolated rural or suburban area. Peace of mind needs to be quantified somehow for both yourself and your family. Factors for analysis should include crime, proximity to work, retail services nearby, and entertainment. You will also want to check on how closely you match the prevalent demographic in the area. If you are a young college graduate, chances are you don't want to live in an established suburban area where the average age is 65.

Establish a questionnaire to include all the pros and cons of where you might want to live. Time spent on researching this decision, will better prepare you while minimizing unexpected surprises. Again, this is an analysis that should be reviewed with the support of your personal board of directors. Having discussions with others regarding their prior experiences will certainly be useful when completing your planning analysis.

Transportation

Closely related to well-being is transportation. How will you be getting around? What is the cost of such transportation? How convenient is it and how much will it cost? With transportation disrupters such as Uber and Lyft, automobile ownership is going through a radical shift—especially for those working and living in metropolitan areas.

Your analysis in transportation should include all associated costs such as car payments, insurance, maintenance, fuel and when it comes to city living, and expenses associated with parking. Shockingly, these total costs can be extremely high, depending on where you live.

To appreciate how much your place of residence can affect transportation costs, just look at the price of gas in the state of California. At one point in 2019, the cost of gas in San Diego was a mind boggling $5 per gallon, which by comparison was significantly higher than the state average of $3.63. To make matters even worse, the national average for fuel per gallon was

$2.60![56] The state of California is becoming known as "the Petro State" rather than the Golden State.

You will also want to consider alternative public transportation options such as buses and subways. Walkability to work, groceries, restaurants, and entertainment venues are also an important consideration. In your analysis, encompass some "what-if" scenarios to quantify the costs associated with not having a car in certain situations such as dates, work-related travel, and visiting friends and family. This will help you to establish a financial roadmap.

Be mindful that if you decide you must buy a car, be wise. The rapidly increasing prices of new automobiles are essentially outpacing the ability of the middle class to afford them. With the continual improvement in safety features, technology, multimedia displays, and overall driving experiences, inflation in car prices has significantly outpaced wage growth over the past decade.

When these things happen, financial engineering always comes to the consumer's rescue. In this case, it

---

[56] Amrith Ramakumar. "Rising California Gasoline Prices Highlight Growing Divide In U.S. " *Wall Street Journal.* October 23, 2019. https://www.wsj.com/articles/rising-california-gasoline-prices-highlight-growing-divide-in-u-s-11571832001

is in the form of historically low interest rates and extended lending terms which currently can approach upward of nine years. In the past, a general guideline when buying a car is that your car payment should not exceed 10% of your gross income. However, today's inflated automobile prices have made purchasing out of reach for most younger middle-class buyers who, in the past, would finance such purchases for only three to five years.

Based on data from Experian, the average auto loan has grown to over 30% of gross income and at an estimated cost of $32,119.[57] Current loan terms have had to be extended from 36-60 months to as much as 72-98 months to afford a similar monthly car payment from a decade earlier. [58]

If you think most people would never consider going out to such term lengths, Experian reported that around one-third of all auto loans taken in the first half of 2019 had longer than six-year terms. On top of that, 1.5% had loans of 85 months or longer. [59]

---

[57] Matt Tatham. "Auto Loan Debt Sets Record Highs." *Experian.* July 18, 2019. https://www.experian.com/blogs/ask-experiamn/research/auto-loan-debt-study/

[58] Ibid.

[59] Ibid.

As late as 2015, there were no such thing as eight- or nine-year automobile loans. The Federal Reserve estimates that there is currently $1.3 billion of debt associated with automobiles (not too far from student debt) and that is almost double the $740 million of car debt from a decade earlier.[60]

If you need a car, take the time to plan and analyze the why, what, and how of such a purchase. Remember that new car you are considering financing over five, seven, or even eight years will start to depreciate as soon as you drive it off the lot. Minimize the emotional investment associated with the car! Do not put yourself under financial stress unnecessarily, especially when you are just starting out.

You may be doing yourself a huge favor by researching and finding a used car that is appropriate for your needs. If you live in the north in an area that gets snow every year, finding a used car that has AWD is a far more practical way to go than a new rear wheel drive sports car. Such a vehicle will also drain your wallet

---

[60] Ben Eisen, Adrienne Roberts. "The Seven-Year Auto Loan; America's Middle Class Can't Afford Their Cara." October 1, 2019, *Wall Street Journal*. https://www.wsj.com/articles/the-seven-year-auto-loan-americas-middle-class-cant-afford-their-cars-11569941215

with insurance costs, especially if you live in a city and are relatively young.

Healthcare Facilities

I know anyone under 30, and maybe even 40, who is reasonably healthy is going to protest and say they are never sick. However, before you skip this section, be forewarned that eventually some unexpected issue will hit you when you least expect it.

My son Adam learned that lesson the hard way in Boston when he thought he had strep throat. He went to the emergency room without giving it much thought. A doctor looked him over and in less than five minutes, determined he had a bad cold and charged him $1,500 more than what his insurance covered.

Upon the advice of his personal board of directors (Mom and Dad), he negotiated the amount down to around $900, which he paid over 10 months. Not surprisingly he learned a valuable lesson. As a result, he identified several walk-in medical clinics and pharmacies that could treat him at a fraction of the cost.

Be prepared. As part of your planning, include a few what-if medical scenarios that will identify where the nearest hospital, medical clinics, and pharmacies are located.

It is also very important that you spend the time necessary to fully understand the medical insurance options available through your employer. One of the first things you will want to determine is whether your nearby doctors, pharmacies, and walk-in clinics are "in or out" of your insurance coverage's network. In versus out of network is a huge determining factor in what you will pay for medical care.

Additionally, review your company's health insurance options. In addition to group medical insurance, your employer may provide additional choices in the form of Flex Spending Accounts and/or a Health Savings Account (HSA). An HSA is a tax-advantaged medical savings account available to taxpayers in the United States who are enrolled in a high-deductible health plan (HDHP).

Funds contributed to this account are not subject to federal income tax at the time of deposit. Unlike a flexible spending account (FSA), HSA funds roll over and accumulate year after year if not spent. HSAs are owned by the individual and are portable if you move from one job to another. Funds may be used to pay for qualified medical expenses at any time without federal tax liability or penalty. An HSA may or may not be appropriate for you based on your age and health, among other factors. However, if such an option is offered, utilize the company's benefits department and your personal board of directors to educate you on the pros and cons of this option.

Spend time obtaining this information and review it annually during enrollment. Keep it available for when you eventually will need it. Health care insurance costs have been the angst of American businesses for decades. From the time that I was the CFO at one of the largest privately owned NH retailers, back in the mid-1990s, rising health care costs have remained a major issue. Over the decades, health care inflation has risen dramatically compared to wages in general. It is gotten to the point that companies have had to steadily increase the portion they pay for your insurance. Today that trend continues.

According to the 2019 Benchmark Kaiser Family Foundation (KFF) Employer Health Benefits Survey, employer sponsored health insurance rose 5% to an average of $20,576.[61] In comparison for the first half

[61] Joyce Blay. "Worker Health Premiums Now Topping $20K Year." October 1, 2019. *Financial Advisor Magazine.*

of 2019, wage inflation rose 3.4% and overall inflation rose 2%, continuing the ongoing trend. [62]

What is the overall impact for an employee? Although companies may still pay the majority of a worker's single insurance premium, more of the obligation is falling to the employee, with an average employee contribution for family coverage at approximately $6,015.[63] If that sounds like a significant amount to you, it is. Since 2009, wage inflation has increased approximately 26% while health insurance premiums for a family have increased 54% and an employee's contribution for this coverage has increased a whopping 71%![64]

To add insult to injury (pun not intended), employees have seen further increases in costs as deductibles and co-pays rise, and more coverage exclusions appear—resulting in additional financial burdens on the employee. Increasing deductibles is currently in vogue to supplement Health Savings Accounts, which aim to stem rising costs by utilizing high deductible catastrophic insurance plans.

---

62 Ibid.
63 Ibid.
64 Ibid.

This premise is further supported by data from the KFF survey, which indicated that 1 in 8 covered employees have a deductible of at least $3,000![65] Someone who turns 26 and is no longer on their parent's coverage could be looking at significant insurance costs as a percentage of their gross income. This is certainly a tough pill to swallow (pun intended).

Social Network and Quality of Life Proximity

From a life-balance and an emotional well-being perspective, how geographically close you are to friends, family, and entertainment are all important factors to consider. Establishing a healthy social network is key to mental, physical, and emotional rejuvenation outside of work. Afterall, we are not robots.

Working hard at the first job only to go home and spend leisure hours gaming because your social network is far away is not exactly a recipe for a healthy lifestyle. Even if that is your thing, you still need an avenue for social interaction. I do not want to belabor the point, but please do not minimize the importance of

[65] Ibid.

the impact of this on your overall success and happiness.

Choosing that first job out of college in a major milestone. You can see that there is far more to making a wise employment decision than just salary. It is important to look at the employment package as just that—a package—and evaluate the value of the complete package including benefits and other potential perks.

It is equally as imperative to consider life-balance issues and have clarity on what is most important to you. Develop your personal questionnaires and consult your board of directors to help you with new challenges along the way. When you do this, you are setting yourself up for success, beginning with your first real career choice.

Chapter 3 Action Steps

1. Create an excel spreadsheet for surveying the various points of consideration outlined in this chapter.

2. Go to jaylevyplanning.net or request at **jaylevyplanning@gmail.com** to download interactive budget form and start completing it once you have an idea of what job and location you are considering. Work with local contacts to obtain estimates on current and expected additional expenses you may be facing, and compare it with the estimated net compensation (net of estimated taxes, benefits, etc.) Go to jaylevyplanning.net to download Annual Key Financial Data, which will provide guidance regarding taxes, retirement contribution allowances, and more. This is an essential exercise that requires sufficient attention to minimize potential surprises!

3. Once established, develop a network of social, community and industry contacts.

Some of these newly established contacts may potentially be future add on to your personal advisory board of directors.

4. Continue to embrace learning (technology, and non-job related) and possible volunteer opportunities within your community or company.

CHAPTER 4

Married With Children

Each phase of life brings with it new and different opportunities as well as unique challenges. By now, you have graduated from college and landed that first job. The next phase typically involves finding your significant other and with that, the possibility of children. Both represent major life changes and require candid financial conversations and planning.

Now at this point you're probably thinking "Whoa...hold on! You're moving too fast with your narrative here! Before anything like that happens, we have to make it through the getting a dog-cat-or-goldfish phase of the relationship."

I cannot disagree. However, for the purposes of this book, I am going to bypass the usual path and get right into the major life decisions of relationships. Not that bringing Spike home is not major. It is—just not quite as high on the significance scale as little Tommy or Mary.

Everyone is looking for a special someone that they feel they are compatible with physically, mentally, and emotionally. However, it is just as important to determine if you are financially compatible before making a major commitment. Why? The Institute for Divorce Financial Analysts did a study and found money issues to be the third leading cause of divorce in this country.[66] And, in a *Divorce Magazine* poll, money and children were found to be the two most common reasons cited in divorce proceedings.[67]

Financial Compatibility

Regardless of whether you choose to marry or live together, it is wise to have a several serious financial conversations before you make any long-term decisions. So, what determines if you are financially compatible or not?

---

[66] "Survey: Certified Divorce Financial Analysts Reveal The Leading Causes of Divorce," Accessed January 10, 2020, https://institutedfa.com/Leading-Causes-Divorce.
[67] Ibid.

Your attitude and money mentality play a huge part in how you and your potential partner view and approach money. Money mentality can often be traced back to a person's background and upbringing. If you were brought up in a household where money was always tight, your approach to money will likely be quite different than someone who grew up in a home where money was never an issue.

As your relationship progresses over time, do not avoid such discussions. It is imperative that you work through this part of the discovery process together. And do it before either of you make any serious commitments such as moving in together.

It is also a good idea that you meet the family and try to understand the family's relationship with money. It may help you understand your partner's thoughts and feelings about money.

It is also a good idea to evaluate your upbringing and examine how it has affected your own relationship with money. Was it used to bring happiness, fear, pain, envy, or never even discussed when you were growing up? Understanding your financial upbringing may help explain your behavior relative to stress, anxiety, addiction, or lack of self-confidence.

These conversations tend to accelerate the "learning about each other" stage of the relationship. They can also grow your relationship to a whole new maturity level—one you both may find attractive and intriguing.

It is important to determine where you and your partner fall on the savings/spending continuum. This can be a huge determining factor in your financial compatibility. In fact, I have seen more disagreements around this point than almost any other.

Money can be a very emotional issue. Say for instance that you are a strong saver and your partner is a mighty spender. Reaching common ground can be a challenge because you've each spent a lifetime developing your individual money habits. They can be very difficult to re-learn and the truth is, many people have no desire to do so—regardless of the circumstances.

To determine your financial compatibility, use the following questions to begin the conversation:

- Do you consider yourself a spender, saver, or a combination? Why?
- What are your top financial goals for the next one, three, five, and ten-year period?

- How much debt do you currently have? What kind of debt?
- Do you have a plan for paying your debt down?
- How much do you have in savings?
- Do you contribute to your 401(k) or 403(b)?
- What percentage of your income do you contribute?
- Do you have any other investments?
- Are any of your bills currently past due?
- What do you consider your greatest financial strength? Weakness?
- What are your financial expectations of each other?

Some of these questions may seem bold to you, but it is better to ask them now, than be broadsided with unexpected financial surprises later. If you are considering a long-term relationship, these are all important questions to ask and it is wise to do so.

Once you have worked through these questions with your partner, the next step is to determine in what areas the two of you may be able to find some common ground for compromise. I cannot emphasize enough how important it is to have this conversation before you make a long-term commitment because this is just your foundation. The financial issues you will face will only get more complicated as you progress through life.

Another area you must discuss is the comingling of funds and developing a budget. One of the safest options to begin with is to each maintain your separate bank accounts and have a joint account that you use to pay household bills. You can always comingle funds as your relationship develops and matures.

Creating a budget is not typically the way most of us would care to spend a Saturday. However, because so many people are operating under budgetary restraints of some sort, it is imperative that you develop one. It does not have to be perfect, but you should take it very seriously.

Do not write it out on a napkin that will eventually disappear between the sofa cushions only to be discovered years later by a new owner. They may believe they have found some 21st century time capsule, only to discover what they have stumbled upon is someone's half-hearted efforts to gain control over their financial life.

Do not intellectually cheat yourself on this exercise. It is a habit that, once acquired, will serve you well for the rest of your life. If budgeting for two, it is important that you hold each other accountable to whatever budget to which you agree to.

The first rule of any budget is to always pay yourself some money, off the top, that goes into at least a couple saving buckets. Contributing to your company's 401k account is always a top priority. If your employer provides a match, then take full advantage of this amount. This is free money to you and represents a significant return on each dollar you save before any market performance takes place.

Your second priority and saving bucket is your emergency fund. Having enough liquid savings to cover 6-12 months of expenses should be the eventual goal of everyone. It will not happen in a day, but by saving a dollar at a time, you will eventually get there. The benefit of getting there is a less stressful environment, should something unexpected occur, such as a job loss. Again, to reiterate, developing these habits while you are young will serve you well throughout your life.

Children

The topic of whether to have children is something that should be discussed early in a serious relationship. Having children changes everything.

"In the excitement of parenthood, it's hard to focus on how that little bundle of joy will affect your bottom line," says Ann Dowd, CFP®, vice president at Fidelity, and mother of three. "But a little planning early on can go a long way. Understanding your cash flow, from the time you start your family, is critical to your ability to meet the growing expenses of raising children—and save for your future, too."[68]

Raising a child from birth through age 17, not including college is expensive. A baby born in 2015 can expect to pay between $233,610 to $372,210 according to the U.S. Department of Agriculture (USDA).[69] A four-year public college will add $83,080 to the cost of raising a child, and if you're considering a private college, it could add up to $187,800.[70]

---

[68] "Got Kids? 6 Ways to Manage Costs." *Fidelity.* February 20, 2019. https://www.fidelity.com/learning-center/personal-finance/college-planning/managing-costs-raising-child

[69] Ibid.

[70] Ibid.

In addition to the quantitative cost, the qualitative aspects of having children should also be considered and discussed. The more you and your partner educate yourselves on all aspects of parenting, the fewer bumps in the road you will likely experience. It is important to understand that your life after children will go from it is all about "us" to it's all about "them." This can be a stressful and difficult transition. Plan on discussing the idea of having children in depth.

Geographic Considerations

In addition to affordability and lifestyle, distance from family can take on new importance when children are brought into the picture. It can be extremely helpful to have an extended support system nearby, especially if both you and your partner continue to work in your careers.

Day care can be a significant cost that must be factored into your budget. Having grandparents or other extended family nearby can be critical to reducing the financial stress of starting a family together. In addition to easing financial strain and reducing stress, there can be significant social benefits of different generations of family members participating in the early childhood years.

From the time my two sons, Grant, and Adam, were babies until their later years of high school, they spent most of their summer vacation in Park Rapids, MN, at my wife's parents' Long Lake compound. They were usually joined by their twin cousins, Katherine and Alex who came up from Dallas, TX and later cousins Griffin and William from Edina, MN. The kids enjoyed a summer camp-like experience with their grandparents who realized their life-long dream of being able to watch their grandchildren grow into adulthood. Those summers with grandparents and cousins not only produced lifelong memories but were beneficial for all!

If children are part of your future, it is paramount that you shift your thinking from one level to perhaps a completely different one. Deciding where to live may require a reassessment of prior attractive geographic considerations such as proximity to local microbreweries and restaurants. These may have to take a backseat to the quality of school districts and availability of day care centers. Costs and affordability of housing, transportation, childcare, and proximity to family are all factors to consider when determining which neighborhoods to focus on in your home search.

Dedicate enough time to researching not only the quality of the public education system but also the quality of life wherever you are considering laying down roots during these important years. For those people who do not, the consequences can become a domino effect of negative repercussions.

Imagine deciding to purchase a residence because you can get more land, or a nicer, larger home with no regard to the quality of the public-school district and the safety of the area. Consequences of such poor planning can result in substantial financial costs such as sending kids to a private school and the emotional toll of constant concern over your family's wellbeing.

Also be cognizant of current events and their potential effect on you personally. For instance, a declining automobile manufacturing industry could have dire consequences for areas like Flint, MI. Chances are you wouldn't be too thrilled if you settled in an area that turned out to be destitute for many years to come even if you yourself were fortunate enough to be employed.

Taking the time (yes, I know this is painful) to become involved in community affairs and town budgetary planning sessions can certainly provide somewhat of a crystal ball when it comes to the future of a town. Stronger community involvement could possibly have saved cities, like Stockton, CA, from falling into bankruptcy and despair due to poor financial management.

Deciding to have children is probably the largest time and financial commitment you will ever make in life. The more planning you can do prior to conception, the easier that transition will be from both a time and financial perspective.

Decisions on how to fund your child's education should be made as early in their life as possible. Setting up 529 plans, entering specific state programs if available, depending on FASB applications and loans or some combination of these can all be viable options for this potential major expense. Are grandparents financially able and willing to contribute? If so, in what form and how much?

The answers to these questions often have a direct impact on how much you and your partner can save for retirement, build an adequate emergency fund, or both. Prior and adequate planning can significantly minimize unexpected issues and surprises when it comes to children and other major life decisions. The more you plan, the more stress you and your partner will manage to alleviate throughout your life.

Other Considerations

Deeper conversations about future dreams, goals, and expectations should happen in the beginning and throughout your lives together. Will one of you be the primary breadwinner or do you both have long-term career aspirations? How will that change when you decide to have children?

Balancing children and career can be a challenge. From a logistical standpoint, you may find working opposite shifts may be an option for reducing childcare costs and adding to the quality of your child's life. Another option may be for one of you to transition to a more consultative career where you can work from home. Again, proper planning can save not only money but can give your relationship the greatest opportunity for success.

Health care is another area to consider when making major decisions, especially when children are involved. Millennials are currently the largest segment of the U.S. population, and, as such, are shaking up the healthcare industry.

Millennial mindsets relative to healthcare and healthcare delivery are very different from traditional healthcare models, which will be forced to adapt to accommodate their changing habits. For instance, while past generations tended to see primary care physicians first, 34% of millennials utilize retail clinics and 24% prefer acute care clinics.[71]

They are also twice as likely to act on health advice they find on the internet. Millennials also embrace high-tech solutions to healthcare.[72] In fact, they have been the driving force behind the increase in wearable medical sensors coupled with apps to monitor data.

Millennials also view healthcare from a more holistic perspective. They rely more heavily on daily health maintenance choices over regular office visits and exams.

Although Millennials are changing the healthcare industry and how healthcare is delivered, one factor remains the same. You always want to search out and budget for the best possible healthcare you can afford for you and your family.

Another important area to consider as you start a family is estate planning. Expectant parents absolutely

---

[71] "7 Ways Millennials Are Changing The Healthcare Industry And What It Means To You)," Accessed January 19, 2020. https://www.team-hfa.com/news/insights/7-ways-millennials-are-changing-healthcare-industry

[72] Ibid.

need a will and revocable trust established to address the "what ifs" of life.

For those who think that estate planning is just for people with a significant amount of money, let me share a story that occurred a while back with someone who was about to become a client. While obtaining background information, I was told that the parents were "all set" because they had a will that they had drawn up more than ten years earlier.

I was immediately concerned because they mentioned only having a (very dated) will. Generally, depending on how much life changes, having such a dated document without a trust is a red flag. Even the most basic estate planning, should address these seven issues:

1. Guardianships should be in place for minor or disabled children. They should include both a primary and a backup choice. They can also provide future directives for naming older children who are currently minors to take on the responsibilities for their younger siblings when they reach a certain age.

2. Be certain that lifetime decisions can be made in case you become mentally impaired or unable to make decisions for yourself. This includes establishing durable powers of attorney for both health and financial decisions, so family members do not have to go to court to obtain guardianship. Establish a living will to address end of life issues that may present themselves. Again, name a primary and a backup choice for each document. Remember also, that because you are dealing with highly emotional events, you may want to consider having multiple people decide (with a tiebreaker always in place) to minimize the potential for stress or guilt tied with one person being responsible.

3. Be sure that whatever assets you have acquired are being passed onto heirs in the most efficient way. This will require discussions and education concerning the various methods assets can be passed, including beneficiary designations on qualified accounts such as 401Ks and IRAs, by operation

of law such as through wills and trusts or by joint ownership with rights of survivorship.

4. Make sure that any federal or state estate taxes are addressed with a plan in place to reduce or eliminate these taxes. Additionally, your attorney, accountant, and advisor should be prepared to discuss the tax ramifications of passing tax qualified investments such as: 401Ks, IRAs, SEPs, 403Bs, Roth IRA or Roth 401K, 457, and Keoghs, among others.

5. Know the most efficient way of passing along a family business.

6. Strategize on protecting assets from long-term care costs, which include long-term care insurance, gifting, life care contracts, and Medicaid planning using life estates and/or irrevocable trusts.

7. Protect yourself against possible lawsuits or other casualties that might endanger your assets while you are still alive. This includes

understanding the following: adequate liability insurance for your home and vehicles, personal umbrella insurance, the best type of entity if you own rental properties, and what types of insurance are appropriate for such assets and for tenants. Also, if you have an interest in a business, know the best entity to operate that business under and again the appropriate insurances to obtain (product liability, premises, errors, and omissions/malpractice). Finally, if you and/or a spouse are in an occupation that has a higher risk for lawsuits, have strategies for protection.

My client and his spouse first and foremost failed number #1 in addressing proper guardianship for their children since their old, outdated will was written two years prior to the birth of their second child. If an unforeseen incident claimed both of their lives, the second child would become a ward of the state they lived in until a court mandated guardianship could be appointed. All because proper planning was not done.

Additionally, it should be noted that when the clients did sit down with their estate planning attorney, they determined that the original assigned guardian for their 10-year-old had to be changed since they'd had a falling out with that person a number of years earlier. The moral of this part of the story is that you should periodically review such important directives because life is constantly changing.

You may not view estate planning discussions as a priority when you are just beginning a life together. However, it is important that you each take steps to protect each other from the financial devastation that can accompany an unexpected or premature death. It is wise to have in-depth discussions with your partner on who you want to be executor of your will.

When children are involved, estate planning discussions become even more important. Who will be the guardian of your children should you and your partner die while your children are still minors? How will assets be overseen for the benefit of your children until they are of legal age? What can you do to protect your child from blowing through all their money?

I realize that no one likes to discuss or plan for their own death. However, these discussions are critical in protecting your family from tragedy. Make sure that any qualified assets or life insurance name the beneficiaries—properly identifying them within the Primary Beneficiary and Contingent Beneficiaries categories.

Be sure to have the proper safeguards in place to handle the asset disposition of the estate in case both spouses become deceased simultaneously.

If you get nothing else from this chapter, get this. Planning today minimizes unexpected surprises tomorrow. As previously mentioned, life decisions only become more complicated as we get older. Acquiring these planning habits will help to reduce some of the stress and anxiety associated with "this life and death stuff."

Try to identify all the possible "what ifs" of life that you can think of—job loss or job expectations (including the amount of travel), having twins or triplets, physical or behavioral health issues. Do not let life happen to you. The more prepared you are for those inevitable patches of rough water, the smoother your journey will be.

Chapter 4 Action Steps

1. Update your budget or if you have not started one, go to jaylevyplanning.net and download the linked forms. Remember any life changing events (change of jobs, getting married and consolidating some living costs, having a child or two, buying a home, etc.).

2. Consider engaging in a "retirement gap analysis" which should be evaluated every two or three years. Either work with your advisor to have it done, investigate doing it online yourself, or reach out at **www.jaylevyplanning.net** to request one.

3. If having children, see action points at the end of Chapter 1 and start engaging in this process during the coming years.

CHAPTER 5

Navigating the Accumulation Stage

At this juncture in your financial life, your kids are probably in those terrible teenage years and you're starting to think more about your own future. This is a perfect time to do an honest where-am-I-in-life self-assessment. This allows you to absorb lessons from the past, see where you are now, and most importantly, assess the future.

This should not be a purely financial assessment, but rather a comprehensive analysis of where you and your partner stand relative to your dreams, goals, and long-term possibilities. Such an internal "self-audit" can be a healthy reality check while there's still time to adjust your plan and direction.

A full self-assessment should also include your children. Where are they relative to health, both physical and mental? How would you gauge their maturity level? Are they progressing as they should in school? Do they have a strong spiritual foundation?

Now is the time to have candid conversations with your children. This will give you a better understanding as to what the future may hold for them, which, in large part, depends on their degree of self-sufficiency. Is college a good choice for them, or are they better off at a local trade school closer to home?

You will want to determine if they are educationally on pace and progressing normally. If they are not, it is important to work with all available resources to identify the reasons as soon as possible.

Remember, life is always presenting "bumps in the road" that can be worked on together as a family. With the advent of social media, video gaming, streaming, and other technological platforms, distractions are certainly more prevalent over the last decade than they have been in the past. While technology certainly has provided undeniable educational and learning benefits, the "distraction issues" that were mentioned in Chapter 1 can create landmines that promote addictive behavior.

If a child is not embracing his education at an early age, parents should continually keep reaching out to establish a communication channel with teachers and advisors. It is important to determine the reasons for this behavior. The child could be bored with the subject matter or they may not be putting forth the effort because they are lazy. If it is an attention problem, medical assessment may be necessary. The key takeaway here is if you ignore the situation, it will continue and may even escalate. Instead of feeling embarrassed to explore what could be causing this behavior, parents and children should look on it as an opportunity to work and learn together.

This is a family partnership. It is important that parents know where their children's interests lie. It is an opportunity to introduce them to a "connecting process" or game that allows them to see beyond their age as to why this might be important later. This is a key point, so let me give you a couple of examples.

Your children may have about as much interest in the STEM subjects (science, technology, engineering, and math) as you have in video games such as Fortnight, Grand Theft Auto, or The Legend of Zelda. Yes, I am guilty! However, a strong potential parent-child bond develops when you can connect the aspects of a video game to the education needed. As you create strategies in the game, you may find yourself integrating aspects of one or more of the STEM subjects. And suddenly, subjects that were once boring now take on a whole new meaning for all concerned.

Think of it as a Sherlock Holmes mystery that both children and parents try to figure out together. Employing games, video or otherwise, are far more meaningful and fun than trying to introduce someone to the subject cold turkey. You are helping them to develop a process for understanding a subject of interest (whatever that may be) by breaking it down into bite-sized pieces to which they can relate.

When parents and children are fully present and working together to answer mystery questions, magic can happen as children become interested in discovering solutions. For example, a simple question concerning a paper coffee cup can be posed to the group. Why can a paper coffee cup hold hot liquid, but if you make a boat out of paper it will sink? Sounds crazy? The great thing about technology and the internet, is a child or parent can do some quick research and find out the answer to that mystery almost instantly.

Although I am not a STEM expert by any means, answers to that question will involve all four components of STEM, science, technology, engineering, and math. Simple questions can grow into more complicated ones like, why did the *Titanic* sink when it hit icebergs when there are ships now that are specifically made to break through the ice in Antarctica?

Imagine the possibilities of learning these things together. From a parent's perspective, you are enjoying quality time, while opening your child's eyes to a world of discovery. This may just inspire them to enjoy more of what education has to offer.

For parents who do not have the patience to understand the world of video gaming, at least take some time to ask your child about what they are playing. Why does it interest them compared to other games? Determine together how much is a reasonable amount of time for them to be playing each day. This gives your child an opportunity for some healthy self-assessment and, gives them new tools for grasping the concept of "time."

This exercise can begin with how many hours there are in a day. From there you can work into how much time they are spending playing the game and how much time remains for other things. Regardless of their interests—reading, learning, sports, video games—time management is a valuable life skill they will need for the rest of their life.

As mentioned previously, collaborating with your children to develop a healthy, balanced curriculum is essential. This should include education, sports, community service volunteering, and, as they enter the early years of high school, eventually internships or part-time jobs. This will create a socially well-adjusted, more mature individual. The key here is to provide the gentle guidance necessary to ensure that the child is not overwhelmed, creating undo stress and anxiety. Kids should never feel cheated out of their childhood because of overly aggressive schedules.

When your child is approaching 11th grade, it is a good time to have some in-depth conversations with them regarding their interests and their plans for college. Discussions should be open and non-judgmental, and you should ask questions that will help to provide a framework for self-discovery for your child. Let us face it. College is not for everybody. It is important that your child does not feel that they "have to" attend college immediately upon graduating from high school.

There may be no more important period than this for a family. Pushing a child to go to college when they have no interest, are not sure, or are not ready, can be both devastating and costly. Everyone knows college is a huge investment but forcing a child to go can also be costly from an emotional, physical, and mental perspective.

Taking a "gap year" may be the right choice for your child. It is often wise for them to take some time to work and take stock of what may interest them if they decide to pursue additional education. They may also find value in attending a less stressful local community college while they figure out their next steps. This is a less expensive path even if only temporary.

If it is decided that college is in the cards, then parents and children should work together on the application process. Choosing schools that have a strong program in your child's area of interest is the first step. It is also important that you are aware of your child's emotional needs as well. Your child may be ready for college but not ready to be on their own far from home. If there is any question, encourage them to stay closer.

It is a good idea to have your child involved with you in the Free Application for Federal Student Aid (FAFSA) process. These days applying for college can be complicated and this is a great opportunity to teach your child a valuable life lesson. They may end up appreciating the opportunity they have been given more if they understand at least on basic level the numbers behind it.

While some parents may not find it appropriate to disclose to their children the financial information required in calculating the key Expected Family Contribution (EFC), it could be advantageous to view it from a different perspective. Through the process, you are teaching them that money does not grow on trees but you have worked and saved over years so you could afford to help with their education.

It is also an opportunity to introduce them to the concept of inflation and give them a real-world example of how college costs have risen more than wages over the past few decades. By going through this process, you will discover if financial assistance is available. Learning how much EFC a family is entitled to can be an invaluable experience.

Since finding such information is not always easy, having your child involved in this Sherlock Holmes mystery is yet another teaching moment. For those unfamiliar with the process, discovering your EFC may be through a college award letter (should be, but not always contained), or the federal government. The EFC number may vary depending on whether the schools use a financial aid application called a CSS profile.

Details of this process are beyond the scope of this book—just remember that obtaining your EFC number is key to seeing how much you are expected to contribute toward your child's education.

It is also wise to educate yourself on what is "aid or free" and what is "aid in the form of loans" so you have a clear understanding of the true costs. Again, it is important that your child be included in this research, so they understand the real costs of their education both for the family and potentially themselves in the form of student loans. This will help your child better understand and appreciate the cost and value of deciding to pursue any undergraduate or graduate degree.

Parents' Personal Financial Audit: Determining if a "Financial Gap" Exists

Most parents are somewhere between their late-30s to mid-50s when their children are old enough to leave the nest. This is a time to shift gears and begin serious planning for yourself to determine if a "financial gap" exists.

I, too, am shifting gears now to share with you valuable financial and holistic planning processes. Up until this point, you may have been just surviving or trying to navigate the complexities of life. For most, this journey is not necessarily smooth. Whether it includes career changes, divorce, remarriage, family dynamics, or health issues, it probably has not been smooth ride through this life stage.

Where do you stand financially? At this juncture in life an internal assessment of your financial life is a wise move. In this assessment, you will want to establish short, intermediate, and long-term goals. An example of a short-term goal would be establishing an emergency fund to cover essential expenses for the family.

Know how much you are spending each month and take the time to develop a budget. There is no shortcut to this process.

It is important to have enough money in liquid accounts. The amount of money you should have in a liquid savings, checking, or money market accounts varies from individual to individual and really depends on whether both you and your spouse are employed, or there is only one of you. If only one person is working, a general rule of thumb is to have twelve months of liquid savings available in case of job loss. If you are both are employed, six months may be enough.

If two people are working but one is bringing in 80% of the household income, you may want to adjust and keep more than six months in liquid accounts. Likewise, if you are in an industry where your skills are in high demand, less than six months in savings may be adequate. The main goal of having this liquidity is to ensure the family has peace-of-mind in case of an unexpected event such as job loss.

Regarding intermediate goals, saving for a five- to fifteen-year goal is where proper planning can really increase your probability of success. An example of an intermediate goal would be paying off your mortgage early by making additional payments. Other examples would be saving for your child's college education or accumulating enough money to make a significant down payment on a business or income-producing property. These latter two goals are attractive because they could potentially provide future revenue streams to supplement your retirement planning.

A primary and worthwhile long-term goal would be saving for investments that can be utilized at a time, such as when someone decides to retire. Most Americans do the bulk of their saving for retirement through qualified retirement vehicles including 401K, 403B, IRA, SEP, and simple accounts.

Over the last couple of decades, there has been a shift away from defined benefit plans or pensions, which guaranteed a fixed sum would be paid to the recipient. Americans have become responsible for saving for their own retirement through defined contribution plans. The days of having companies take care of their workers in retirement are long gone.

Navigating through the maze of trying to save for long-term goals, as well as short-term and intermediate goals can be difficult. Unfortunately, there is no one-size-fits-all solution. Some parents may believe that saving for their children's education takes priority over saving for an emergency fund and retirement. Others may feel that retirement takes precedence.

A practical solution would be to begin with a barbell strategy with most savings earmarked for the emergency fund and long-term retirement savings. It is always wise to contribute enough to your 401(k) that you cover the employer's full match. Your employer's match is like free money to you. Who does not want free money?

At the same time, you could contribute the remainder to build the necessary emergency fund based on your calculated need. Once you have met the short-term goal, your emergency fund, you can now focus on your other financial goals.

In our holistic planning model, we examine not only what you are "retiring from" but also what you are "retiring with" and "retiring to." We will also look at "why" you want to retire and "if" you want to retire completely or continue to work part-time.

Although we are focusing on the financial aspects of "retiring with," there are holistic or non-financial aspects to also consider, which we will discuss in the next chapter. For the remainder of this chapter however, we will focus on trying to establish a guesstimate of what you will need to never outlive your individual or your family's income stream.

As of the writing of this book, legislative activity in Washington D.C. has changed the rules of retirement. As of January 1, 2020, legislation known as the SECURE Act became law and resulted in several changes to certain areas of retirement planning. Some are beneficial to individuals, but the legislation also involved a major change that the government hopes will increase their ability to collect taxes from non-spousal beneficiaries sooner rather than later.

The government essentially eliminated the Stretch IRA provision which previously allowed qualified assets to be passed from one generation to another while still taking advantage of the tax-deferred growth of assets within the IRA account. The SECURE Act basically ended the stretch IRA for non-spousal beneficiaries, and its ability to shelter inherited income. Under the new law, beginning January 1, 2020, non-spousal beneficiaries are required to withdraw all the funds from an inherited IRA within ten years of the original account owner's death.

With that said, a great process I suggest to younger clients is based on the book, *Paychecks for Life* written by Charlie Epstein, (A/K/A The 401K Coach) . Charlie's process explains in simple terms the importance of saving for retirement (or as Charlie sometimes phrases it "Desirement") through your employer's retirement plan.

Charlie suggests the reader treat their retirement account as their own private company. You can utilize two sources of other people's money to grow your company (retirement account). In his illustration, other people's money (OPM), is in the form of tax deferment of the assets in your retirement plan and your employer's company match, if offered.

The point of this exercise is to get you thinking as an entrepreneur even when working for someone else.

Your ultimate financial goal for retirement requires some basic retirement income planning. Notice I said income planning not investment planning or total asset planning. The earlier in life people come to realize income, not necessarily assets are their life blood the better.

While most of bottom half of Americans' wealth is tied up in their home, that asset is not going to put food on the table. Your retirement assets will be converted to income producing assets when you retire. Financial planning begins with an income estimate of what will be needed at retirement to allow you the lifestyle you wish. This income number should be reviewed and adjusted periodically, at least every few years to see how you are doing.

Once you have an income estimate, the next step is to reduce that number by outside income streams you can count on in retirement. For most, this includes Social Security income. Other outside income streams might include pensions, rental income, or annuity income. These outside income sources should be subtracted from your gross income estimate to give you the net income figure you will need.

By working backward from this figure, you can begin to estimate how much you will need to save to reach your retirement income goal. Calculating this is straight forward. Begin by taking the amount saved to date in your investment account. Next, calculate how much you are saving additionally each year. Assign a rate of return based on your years until retirement, or to keep it a simple and conservative figure for example perhaps between 4% and 6%. Figure out how many more years of expected savings you have prior to retiring.

Once you have an investment portfolio amount, line it up with your estimated income needs (after taxes) to see where you currently stand. This analysis will provide a gauge for determining if you are on track or experiencing a "gap" (hence the term, "gap analysis") in your current savings. Based on the gap, calculators can easily figure out how much additional savings will be needed to close the gap and put you on a path to reach your financial goals.

The key to this exercise is to encourage you to save for the long-term. Epstein's book presents nine principles that will help you to ultimately create "paychecks for life." I will not go into detail on these principles, but it is a good idea to review the list:

- Determine Your "Desirement" Mortgage

- Use Other People's Money to Capitalize Your Business
- Harness the Power of Compound Interest
- Use Technology to Save Automatically
- Manage Risk by Outsourcing
- Control Fees and Expenses
- Guarantee Your Paychecks for Life with Annuities
- Take Advantage of Tax Benefits with a Roth
- Act Like an Entrepreneur

Charlie's outlined principles are logical. First, always think as a self-employed individual when saving for the long-term. Use other people's money (employer and the government) to assist in building your wealth. It is always a good idea to start as early as possible. This allows you to take advantage of the power of compound interest. Put everything on automatic so you do not miss it as much. Use automatic enrollment and automatic escalation to get started and increase contributions. Make sure your portfolio is diversified using mutual funds and Exchange Traded Funds with low cost fees and expenses.

Regarding transitioning your portfolios into annuities at some juncture to create a guaranteed income stream or utilizing a Roth option, these areas of discussion are more tied to a person's personal profile. Always review the risk, rewards, and costs of each strategy.

Now is the time to re-access all these things and more. Waiting until you are in your 60s may be too late to avoid a fate that the premise of this book is predicated on. While obviously the earlier one begins planning the better. This stage of your financial life still represents an opportunity to start building that all-important bridge, which will dictate how the rest of your life may be lived. Drop the ball on this and you may be setting yourself on a path from which there is no recovery and an eventual reckoning.

Questions to ask in your financial assessment:

- Are both you and your spouse working?
- What kind of careers is/are you in?
- What is the growth potential in your current job or career?
- To what age will you be working?
- What levels of stress, happiness, and passion are associated with work?
- Are you working out of enjoyment or necessity until Medicare age?

- Are you both moving in the same direction in terms of satisfaction, or is one being left behind? Is this affecting the partnership?
- If a job or career change is in the cards, would you explore self-employment or continue to work for someone else?
- Is working together as a team a possibility? For example, one person is self-employed while the other has a salary and access to benefits?
- Concerning non-qualified and qualified investments, are you reviewing these at least annually to see how you are tracking vs. your retirement goals?
- Have you reviewed your estimated Social Security benefits? If you are concerned about the viability of Social Security, use 75% of your Social Security benefits estimate in your calculations.
- What other assets have you acquired and what debt is associated with each? Are they income-producing assets?
- What is the likelihood that parents will need financial or emotional support?

- How will this potentially affect your work schedule?

We will discuss your holistic assessment in detail in the next chapter. However, here are a few questions to get you started in your holistic assessment:

- What are your dreams, goals, and aspirations together and separately?
- How are these the same or different from when you were first married?
- Are you still supportive of each other's dreams and aspirations?
- What kind of retirement do you envision?

I would like to touch briefly on budgeting. Your budget is as individual as you are and there is no one-size-fits-all in approach. The one thing I cannot emphasize enough is if you have credit card debt, do everything in your power to eliminate it. Review your progress monthly. Get in the habit of using either cash or a debit card. It will drag you down financially and emotionally in addition to taking a serious toll on your ability to save for retirement.

It is important to properly categorize expenses as fixed, discretionary, or a combination. If expenses are becoming out of control, look for community support options for assistance. Other considerations are negotiating with your larger creditors, such as hospitals who are trying to collect on major expenses.

It all comes down to doing the proper planning now. There is no such thing as too much planning during this stage of your life. It is a time when you're balancing college expenses while starting to get serious about your retirement savings. The planning you do now will determine the kind of retirement you will have later.

Chapter 5 Action Steps

1. At this stage of life, a "personal self-audit" should be performed assessing where you and your spouse are financially. Now is the time to estimate your financial needs relative to your projected retirement date. Use the questions outlined in this chapter to mold a holistic view of retirement and begin to set realistic timelines within your financial planning. Such introspection should be done periodically every few years, or whenever there is a significant life changing event, such as a change of job or career or having an additional child.

2. Personal assessments should be completed with each child while they are still in high school. The earlier the better. Doing these assessments with your child will be important their financial maturation process.

3. Educate yourself on better understanding your money psychology and behavior. Read

books such as “Dollars and Sense” to better understand and tweak your financial philosophy.

CHAPTER 6

Empty Nesters with Retirement in Sight

It's imperative that you regularly assess where you currently stand on your road to financial freedom—and the earlier this becomes a habit, the better. These personal assessments are invaluable as you begin to outline and plan for your retirement.

The first step when beginning your retirement planning is to develop a reasonable estimate of the financial resources you will need to live comfortably in retirement. This figure should be reviewed every couple of years, or whenever there is a major change in your income such as starting a new job, losing a job, having children, or buying a home.

Establishing a budget that includes both fixed and discretionary expenses is a key component of serious retirement planning. No one really likes the idea of a budget but committing to one does not mean you have to give up those daily lattes, weekend visits to local restaurants, or regular annual vacations. What it does mean is you have a clear understanding of what you spend weekly, monthly, and annually, as well as having a handle on whether you are living within your means. Regardless of whether you are 30, 50, or 65 years of age, it's a good idea to know what your net income is and how much you're allocating toward various expenses especially savings, both qualified and unqualified.

While this process may seem overwhelming and complicated, rest assured, it is not. The following discussion offers a step-by-step overview on how to proceed. There are also many online resources that can help you with calculators, obtaining your Social Security estimates, Medicare, and other future considerations.

To streamline this process for you, I have briefly outlined a step-by-step approach to getting started with your retirement planning. This is based on an abbreviated version of *Kiplinger's 7 Steps to a Richer*

Retirement.[73] I would strongly recommend reading this outstanding guide.

Your retirement planning is a process you must own. Over the years, I have seen far too many people procrastinate year after year until suddenly, they are in their 50s or 60s and unprepared for their financial future. Again, the earlier you start the process, the better. However, even if you are starting late, starting at any age is always better than not starting at all.

Planning for a Richer Retirement

Step 1. Complete Kiplinger's Online Retirement Savings Calculator.

This tool can be found at:

https://www.kiplinger.com/tool/retirement/T047-S001-retirement-savings-calculator-how-much-money-do-i/index.php

This calculator helps you estimate how much money will be necessary for you to retire. Based on your answers to some basic questions, it will

73 "7 Steps to a Richer Retirement." *Kiplinger's.* Accessed January 28, 2020. https://store.kiplinger.com/7-steps-to-retirement.html

determine how much income you will need in retirement. It looks at approximately how much retirement income you will receive from Social Security and Pensions, as well as how much retirement savings you have already accumulated. It also takes into consideration, how much money you will be able to draw from home equity. Then, it provides you with a figure of what you will need to retire.

It is important to remember that this approximation is based on your estimated expenses in the future. Remember to revisit these estimates whenever your income or expenses go substantially up or down. Things like a new job, an inheritance, children, grandchildren, and unforeseen medical issues can all affect your retirement calculations and may necessitate you adjusting on your road to retirement.

Once you have estimated your expenses and you are clear on which are fixed and which are discretionary, your next step is determine your anticipated guaranteed income streams. This would include income derived from Social Security, pensions, and annuities. There may be other potential sources such as trust assets from an inheritance, but it is a good idea to remain conservative when estimating outside income sources.

Once all possible income streams are calculated, subtract them from your estimated retirement income figure. What remains is the amount that must be covered by savings, investments (both qualified and non-qualified) and other assets that can produce additional income. Do not forget that taxes will play an important part in this analysis. While no one can predict what individual, local, state, and federal tax rates will look like in the future, it is always best to err on the side of caution and assume they will rise. We will discuss possible tax strategies you may want to consider in this and the following chapters.

A key component in the retirement calculator is estimating what percentage of current income you will want to generate in retirement. While there is no standard guideline, financial advisors often recommend that you cover 70%-80% of your current income in retirement. It is also wise to include an annual inflation factor in 2-4% range. Kiplinger provides a money-growth and inflation factor table that are a great beginning reference point.

Once you know your retirement number, determine what kind of "gap" you are looking at on your current savings path. Unless you fill that gap with additional savings, you may find yourself coming up short when meeting your financial goals.

Step 2. Determine what you will get from Social Security.

Social Security is one potential income stream that most Americans have paid into and are "entitled" to receive. I am being sarcastic when I say "entitled" because you have paid into Social Security for at least ten years and are basically self-funding your own annuity.

Social Security shortfalls arise because what you have contributed to the Social Security Trust has funded the benefits for prior generations. Contributions are not segregated by individual contributor.

The program was established in the 1940s when there was an estimated forty-two people paying into the system to cover each recipient receiving benefits. Over the decades this worker/recipient ratio has declined to a point that in 2018 there are approximately 2.8 workers paying into the system for each person receiving benefits.[74] Also, because of a significantly

[74] "Social Security Recipient to Worker Ratio." *Federal Budget in Pictures*. Accessed February 9, 2020. https://www.federalbudgetinpictures.com/social-security-recipient-worker-ratio/

shorter life expectancy at the time, Social Security was only designed to pay benefits for a few years.

Because of continuing advancements in healthcare, people are living longer, and many are retiring younger. Consequently, the Social Security System is forced to pay benefits over longer and longer periods of time. The amount of benefits paid out now exceeds the amount of money being paid into the system. Principle is now being tapped to supplement annual shortfalls.

If modifications are not made to the current process, the Social Security Trust is estimated to be completely depleted by 2035.[75] A common misconception is that Social Security will not be around for recipients if this occurs. This is untrue. According to Social Security, the more likely scenario is that benefits would be reduced by 25% across the board.[76] Even the likelihood of this happening is relatively small.

---

[75] "The Social Security Trust Fund Will Run Out of Money by 2035." *Barron's*. Accessed February 9, 2020. https://www.barrons.com/articles/social-security-deficit-reserves-check-benefits-payroll-tax-51555958282

[76] Stephen C. Goss. "The Financial Future of the Social Security Program." *Social Security Office of Retirement and Disability Policy*. Accessed February 9, 2020. https://www.ssa.gov/policy/docs/ssb/v70n3/v70n3p111.html

Political pressures will force the government to develop modifications that can extend the program for a few decades. Some possible remedies include raising the FRA (full retirement age) and removing or increasing the cap for taxing Social Security benefits. In 2020, taxing benefits is capped at $137,700.[77] Raising the cap would increase tax revenue to support the Trust. Revising the metrics for calculating COLAs (annual inflation-tied cost of living adjustments) has also been considered.

It is my opinion that some combination of these ideas will probably be used to extend the benefit program without any sort of benefit reduction. The big question is: When? With politicians at the helm, revisions are not likely to come until later—perhaps during elections in 2024 or 2028. In the meantime, plan on estimated benefits as part of your personal planning analysis.

To obtain your estimated benefits, you can go online to www.ssa.gov, establish a username and password and gain access to your annual earnings history, estimated Social Security, and even disability benefits.

[77] Jim Probasco. "6 Social Security Changes in 2020." *Investopedia,* Updated January 24, 2020.
https://www.ssa.gov/policy/docs/ssb/v70n3/v70n3p111. html

A detailed discussion of all the minutia associated with Social Security is beyond the scope of this book. However, I would like to discuss some key points of which you should be aware.

To receive benefits, you must work a minimum of 40 quarters (10 years) and have paid into the program during that period. If you work for a public system or the government and are not required to pay into Social Security, you may be ineligible or have reduced benefits.

Your SS benefits will reflect three estimated payouts, one at age 62, one at FRA (full retirement age), and one at 70 years of age. At FRA, you will receive 100% of your calculated PIA (primary insurance amount). Jump the gun early on Social Security and you are looking at a reduction of approximately 25%, depending on your date of birth. This means over your lifetime you will be paid only 75% of your total benefits.[78] Taking Social Security early is a very expensive decision, and not usually a wise one.

---

[78] Steven Hinden. "How Much Does Early Retirement Reduce Benefits." *AARP*. Accessed February 9, 2020 https://www.aarp.org/work/social-security/info-04-2013/early-retirement-social-security-benefits.html

Delaying payments past your FRA will provide an additional 8% annual increase until you reach age 70.[79] Currently, your birthdate determines your FRA, but you can plan on it falling somewhere between 66 and 67 years of age. Depending on your estimated FRA, you can potentially increase your benefits between 24%-32% by delaying until age 70, which means that over your lifetime, you could collect 124-132% of your total benefits.[80] This can be significant from a planning perspective, but it's a decision that should not be made without a comprehensive personal analysis.

These three payout options were developed so that those who need early access, have a choice, but it comes at a cost—a reduction in benefits. People may decide to turn on Social Security early for any number of reasons—economic, health-related, belief that the system will be insolvent in the future or a combination of these factors. Actuaries have reportedly done the math on these options to determine the breakeven for receiving "reduced but for an increased number of payments over time" versus receiving "increased payment amounts over a reduced period of time."

---

[79]"What Are Delayed Retirement Credits And How Do They Work." *AARP*. Accessed February 9, 2020. https://www.aarp.org/retirement/social-security/questions-answers/delayed-retirement-credits/
[80] Ibid.

Assuming a classic, basic breakeven analysis (assuming no cost of living increases and no investment returns) this breakeven point lies somewhere in the range of 78-80 years. If you die after 78, you basically came out ahead. Living into your 80s or 90s can result in tens or even hundreds of thousands more paid out to you in benefits.[81]

Figuring out when you will take Social Security is an important factor in the financial planning process. You will want to analyze your health, work intent, accumulated savings, investments, and other sources of income, etc. If you are in good health, have a solid family medical history, want to continue working, or have substantial retirement assets, waiting until FRA or age 70 may be the best strategy. If you are married, and your spouse will receive your "survivor" benefits for the rest of their life, the Social Security decision becomes a decision you are making for two.

However, if you are in poor health or need Social Security income for everyday living, taking even a reduced benefit may be the best option. To help determine when taking such payments will affect your benefits, the Social Security Administration has

---

[81] Elaine Floyd. "Savvy Social Security *Course*." *Horsesmouth.* 2020 Edition

calculators that can provide guidance. Go to www.ssa.gov/quickcalc/earlylate.html. If you would like further information on your life expectancy, you can access IRS Publication 590-B under Individual Retirement Arrangements simply visit IRS.gov. Seeking further guidance on this topic? Reach out to me at **www.jaylevyplanning.net** to discuss.

Be sure to do your research before making your Social Security decision. With pensions almost a thing of the past, there simply are not that many guaranteed income streams available. Therefore, Social Security is an important component of your overall financial life.

When you are approximately five to ten years from retirement, you are entering a critical stage, one in which a deeper, more comprehensive personal assessment is needed. Consider this assessment a two-part process. The first is purely financial and the second is non-financial, but just as important to your overall retirement success.

Financial Planning Audit

In your comprehensive financial planning audit, begin by analyzing your financial picture regarding assets. This includes liquid (savings), investments (both qualified and non-qualified), real estate, the lump sum value of pensions and annuities, and any other assets you have earmarked for retirement. Do the same with all liabilities and debt obligations (both short- and long-term). Additionally, a personal cash flow statement should be generated to account for additional savings you anticipate acquiring during the pre-retirement period.

The second part of this financial process is to review your present budget and begin to estimate your expected expenses (along with an associated inflation rate) in retirement. Although you may slow down a bit in retirement, inflation will not.

Once you have an estimate of your anticipated retirement expenses, next you will want to review both your current and future assets relative to the income streams (on an after-tax basis) they are capable of generating in the future. Revisit this analysis on a periodic basis. It is not necessary to do this annually, but you should plan on doing so after any significant life change.

These life changes can be the result of a "planned event" such as retiring, partial retirement, changing careers, turning on social security, becoming eligible for Medicare, buying a business, or even considering a moving to a different part of the country. As we all know, major life changes are often "unplanned events." These can include being laid off from a job, substantial house expenditures, a sudden health issue, and even a significant change in your federal or state tax structure. To avoid surprises, it is wise to include certain "what-if" scenarios such as moving to a different locale, downsizing a home, and other cost-of-living considerations.

I usually recommend that we work on calculating current and projected retirement expenses while in the late accumulation phase of your financial life. It's important that you have adequate time to alter your spending behavior while still working.

What you discover during this "assessment stage," will help you to determine if you can retire with the lifestyle you desire. Keep in mind that this exercise is not necessarily intended to dictate when you will be retiring, but rather where you stand financially at the time of your analysis.

Regarding taxes, it is important to understand the impact different taxes such as capital gains tax and income tax will have on your retirement income. Specifically, you want to be clear on their potential impact on your Social Security and Medicare benefits.

As previously discussed, there is ongoing debate on whether Social Security assets will be depleted sometime around 2035. However, barring an unforeseen economic collapse, there will still be workers contributing, which offers some safety net against a complete elimination of the program.

Unless the system is somehow supported through increased taxes or by amending some internal formulas, the benefit payout could be reduced by an estimated 25% in the future. While this could be devasting to those who rely on Social Security for a large percentage of their retirement income, it is still expected to remain an important income stream for many retiring Americans. If you prefer to err on side of caution, it may behoove you to plan on only collecting 75% of your benefit in retirement.

Medicare remains a moving target. As we move further into 2020, efforts to accurately calculate costs depend on several factors that will undoubtedly change by the time you are ready to retire. Trying to anticipate whether there will be a "Medicare For All" platform in place, a more public health care program with supplemental private insurance still available, or a continuation of the existing program with additional government subsidies is for the bookies in Las Vegas to figure out. However, for those approaching age 65, a more in-depth discussion of what you need to know about Medicare follows in the next chapter.

As you work through your assessment, take this time to review and update your estate plan. Be sure your other financial and health-related durable powers are in place, as well a living trust. When reviewing these documents, determine if any are outdated, or if your intentions have changed over the years.

As you approach 60, it is wise to start researching long-term care quotes. This type of insurance is something most people will need in retirement. Affordability, financial stability of the insurer, and one's current health (to see if you qualify) are all factors to consider.

Non-Financial Audit

The second part of your personal assessment involves the non-financial factors that you must consider ensuring a happy and fulfilling retirement. Although it may be tempting to ignore this part of your assessment, you will find that they are just as important as the financial factors previously discussed. I came to realize just how important non-financial factors are after obtaining the designation, Certified Professional Retirement Coach or (CPRC), which I soon realized was the perfect complement to my Certified Financial Planner (CFP) certification.

When I put on my CPRC hat, I delve much deeper with clients to address their mental and emotional transition into retirement. I cannot emphasize enough the importance of discussing these components, which are often overlooked in the traditional retirement planning process.

Most people have no idea how dramatically their life will change once they retire. There is not another stage in life that evokes the intense emotions that retirement does. Although retirement can be an exciting and liberating time in your life, it can frequently trigger feelings of fear and anxiety.

For many, especially men, a huge part of their identity is tied to their career and what they do for a living. Often when I ask clients what they plan to do in retirement, I get the standard answers—travel, golf, fish, and spend time with family. Let us face it. You can only travel, golf, and fish so much before what was once a great escape from routine, *becomes* routine and boring.

Most retirees report that retirement was not at all what they expected. Virtually every facet of your life changes in retirement. You no longer have the structure to your day that work provided. Often your social network shrinks substantially when you leave your job. It is common for retirees to experience feelings of anxiety, restlessness, and boredom. Retired men are found to be 40% more likely than men in the workforce to experience depression and between 2000 and 2016, the highest suicide rates occurred in men between the ages of 45 and 64.[82]

Even if you were never enamored with your job or career, the jolting exit to retirement can result in a period of "grief" that you must prepared for. Therefore, it is so important to spend time planning out how you want to spend your time in retirement and who you want to be in retirement.

It is also critical that you and your spouse have deep and honest retirement discussions. Remember, suddenly you and your spouse are going to be together 24/7. It is important you are on the same page and have a plan—not to drive each other crazy.

---

[82] "You're Probably Not Ready to Retire – Psychologically." *MarketWatch.* accessed February 15, 2020. https://www.marketwatch.com/story/why-youre-probably-not-psychologically-ready-to-retire-2019-05-21

Although many people have planned for retirement their entire adult life, I can't tell you how many times I've had couples come into my office, never having discussed, except in very general terms what they plan to do in retirement. I remember one couple in particular—when I asked what they wanted to do in retirement, the husband immediately said he wanted to travel. The wife was shocked and responded that she traveled her entire career for work. The last thing she wanted to do was travel! This not something you want to discover on retirement day.

Many times, clients do not know where to begin to address the non-financial planning aspects of retirement. Typically, I start by having clients develop a Values List. This is simply a list of what is most important to them in retirement. I have couples complete their list separately before we discuss the lists and begin to merge them into one. Once you know what is most important to you and your partner, you are in a good position to discuss the specifics.

Next, I have them create a Curiosity List. This is a list of all the activities they are curious about and would like to research or explore in more detail. Depending on your personal Curiosity List, some of these activities can not only expand your mind but also your social network, which, as I mentioned previously, may take a hit when you leave your job. This list can also be the start of replacing your work identity with a new one of your own choosing.

Retirement can potentially be the longest phase of your life. It can also be the most extraordinary stage as well. However, it requires proper planning well in advance of your retirement date. Obviously, financial planning is an essential part of the process to ensure you do not run out of money. However, non-financial planning is essential to the quality of your everyday life in retirement.

All too often, people view retirement as an ending. However, with proper planning it can be an exciting new beginning when you can become the person you've always wanted to be and do the things you always wanted to do but couldn't because other aspects of life got in the way.

Chapter 6 Action Steps

1. At this stage, a deeper assessment is in order regarding the financial and non-financial aspects of planning. This exercise should be easier since you are now closer to certain timelines such as Social Security, Medicare, and potential retirement or semi-retirement dates. At this juncture, you should also have greater clarity concerning non-financial aspects of your planning. Now is the time to begin to transition your thinking from what you are "retiring from" to what you're "retiring with and to." For some useful complimentary tools for providing some guidance in this analysis, go to **www.jaylevyplanning.net**

2. If you are currently healthy with a reasonably decent family medical history, plan on including a revised budget that considers the present and future costs that will take you to 100 years of age. Look at current personal tax rates and evaluate potential

changes that could impact you. Always err on the side of caution and it's wise to have a worst-case scenario plan in place.

3. Develop a distribution strategy with your advisory team. Potential landmines surrounding sequential risks, tax planning, and bucket strategy formations should all be discussed. If you do not work with a financial advisor, accountant, and estate attorney consider reaching out to me on my website, **www.jaylevyplanning.net** or email **jaylevyplanning@gmail.com** to discuss.

CHAPTER 7

Social Security, Medicare, & Distribution of Assets

Over the years, many books have been written about how to get up Mt. Everest but, have you ever noticed that there are very few books penned about how to get down? Although most problems and fatalities occur on the way down Mt. Everest, you would be hard pressed to find even a handful of books that go into detail on how to return safely from the summit. I tell my clients all the time that some advisors probably have the knowledge and skill to get you up the mountain. However, getting you down the retirement mountain safely and without running out of money takes expertise and a very specific skill set.

In the last chapter, you identified your values and your curiosity list (if not, for guidance, go to www.jaylevyplanning.net). You know what is most important to you and your spouse as you enter retirement and you know the activities you would like to explore further. Upon completing both the financial and non-financial components of your holistic planning personal assessment, we now have a concrete direction and can begin to make decisions about which income streams should be turned on when as you proceed through retirement.

At this juncture we will also discuss everything you need to know about Medicare. I will outline what it covers and what it costs, as well as the supplemental coverages you'll have to purchase to cover gaps in coverage due to medical exclusions, deductibles, co-pays, and related costs. Medicare supplements or Medigap insurance can mean significant additional costs on an annual basis.

When evaluating your potential retirement income streams, there are three key areas you must explore. First, we must look at the total retirement savings you have managed to accrue over your lifetime. This determines how much financial freedom you will have to experience everything you would like to experience in retirement. Second, the non-financial aspects of considering full or partial retirement needs to be fully analyzed as previously discussed. Failure to do this may have significant repercussions that you can never repair. Finally, your current state of health also plays a big role in how you will spend your retirement days.

If your savings are minimal and a large part of your retirement income will be from your Social Security benefits, your choices will be limited. You either must continue working for as long as you are physically and mentally able, or live a life of frugality, and, in some cases, possibly outright poverty. There is no "nice "way of putting it. This is the point in time when your prior life choices can come back to haunt you.

Therefore, I recommend everyone read through this book, regardless of age. My goal in writing it is to try to prepare you as early and as often as I can, so that you are able to avoid the hopeless scenario above. As you navigate through life, you will experience both planned and unplanned events that can throw you off your financial course. These may include decisions early in your life such as cashing in investments or retirement savings to pay off student, auto or credit card debt. No matter what life throws you, it is wise to make decisions with both the present and future in mind.

My son, Grant, offers a perfect example of having to weigh present consequences versus the future potential in his decision to pursue post-graduate studies. He accumulated around $20,000 in student debt while obtaining his undergraduate degree in chemical engineering. The master's degree he wanted to earn in computer science was going to add an additional $40,000, meaning he would owe a total of $60,000 by the time he graduated with his master's.

The loans would carry about a 6% interest rate. His dilemma was should he cash in his approximate $10,000 of savings and $21,000 of non-qualified investments to pay down the debt? He was further conflicted because he enjoyed a 25% return on his investments during the 2019 year.

What relevancy does Grant's story at age 26 have to this discussion? There are going to be major life decisions on everyone's life journey. Some of these will define who we are and what we have become decades later in life. Your ability to connect these dots throughout your financial life is one of essential points of this book.

Grant believes his master's degree will lead to future opportunities that will utilize his engineering and programming education. However, the initial pain of additional debt is a reality in the present. He's betting that his master's degree equates to an increase in earnings that can offset some of the financial burden of additional debt and allow him to live a balanced, enjoyable life while also continuing to save for the future. If you can't say with some degree of certainty that such a personal investment will pay similar benefits, then perhaps, you should re-assess your options from a financial perspective.

There will be always be non-financial variables that play into decisions such as these. However, it is important to always weigh the financial risk/rewards accordingly. The culmination of these decision points ultimately leads to the degree of financial freedom you can enjoy in retirement.

Whether or not to have children is another one of those key decision points in life. As I pointed out in earlier chapters, the decision to have two or three children can be an expensive one, costing approximately $200,000-$400,000 each (excluding secondary education expenses). In most cases, this is a small price to pay for the love and enjoyment of having children but making a conscious decision of having children without taking the time to fully understand the cost involved is just poor planning.

Medicare

Health care costs in the U.S. are completely out of control. For those who are approaching their mid-60s, health care will likely be their greatest, ongoing expense. Unfortunately, when they started saving for retirement, they had no idea how large, fast-growing, and complicated retirement health coverage would become. Because it is an increasingly growing drain on retirement income, it is a key factor that must be addressed in your financial planning.

From 1965 to 1985, health care costs tripled in real (inflation-adjusted) terms from $187 billion to $666 billion. And then, over the next twenty years, spending nearly tripled again to $1.9 trillion in 2005. Over the last thirteen years (to 2018) that figure ballooned to an estimated $3.65 trillion.[83] It is like a black hole sucking everyone into its void: corporations, governments, and individuals. And regarding individuals or specifically you and your spouse, a Fidelity Analysis estimates a 65-year-old couple will need $280,000 to cover health

---

[83] Kimberly Amadeo. "The Rising Cost of Health Care by Year and It's Causes." *The Balance.* Updated February 28, 2020. https://www.thebalance.com/causes-of-rising-healthcare-costs-4064878

care and medical expenses throughout retirement.[84] This figure represents a 75% increase over their initial estimate of $160,000 when their initial analysis commenced back in 2002.[85]

Although, in-depth discussion of Medicare is beyond the scope of this book, I have provided some points you should know as you make your Medicare decisions. Early in 2020, Democratic political primaries are in full swing with many of the candidates proposing "Medicare For All" or some version of increasing government subsidies while minimizing or eliminating private insurance options.

I do my best to avoid any political bias. One thing that both parties can agree on is the required subsidy will likely cost many trillions of dollars over a two-year period. Regardless of where this money may come from, there is little question that the tax structure for individuals will have to be amended to afford this kind of additional spending.

Remember—everything connects in life. Costs associated with increasing health care coverage and

[84] "A Couple Retiring in 2018 Would Need an Estimated $280,000 to Cover Health Care Costs in Retirement, Fidelity® Analysis Shows." *Fidelity.* April 19, 2018. https://www.fidelity.com/about-fidelity/employer-services/a-couple-retiring-in-2018-would-need-estimated-280000
[85] Ibid.

subsequent tax code changes, will necessitate adjustments in your financial planning. Financial planning is a moving target, which is why your financial plan should be reviewed periodically and adjusted as situations change.

Medicare Parts

Medicare is comprised of different parts which cover different segments of healthcare. Medicare Part A covers a portion of the cost of hospitalization. Part B partially covers doctor visits and other healthcare services. Part D covers drugs and is available through private insurers.

The most common misconception about Medicare is that it covers all your healthcare costs. Medicare pays first and supplemental insurance is designed to pay what Medicare does not.

However, Part D works differently because it is only available through private insurers who have a contract with Medicare. Your first step is to find an insurer in your area that offers a Medicare drug plan. Each drug plan has its own list of covered drugs, different coverages, and different pricing. Although you can't possibly know what drugs you may need in the future, when you're shopping for Medicare drug plans, be sure you have a list of drugs you are currently taking, the dosages and how much you pay for them now. Find a plan that covers the drugs you take now at the best price available. Shopping Medicare drug plans is a big part of enrolling in Medicare.

Medicare Costs

Another popular misconception about Medicare is that it is free. If you or your spouse had Medicare taxes deducted from your paycheck for at least ten years, then Part A of your monthly premiums are free. However, if you are hospitalized, you'll have to meet a deductible before Medicare pays. If you are in the hospital for more than sixty days, part or all of the daily rate will be your responsibility.

Everyone pays for Part B except those qualifying for special assistance. Your Medicare premium is automatically deducted from your Social Security benefit. If you have not started your Social Security, you will be responsible for the monthly premium. In addition to the premium, you must meet your deductible before Medicare begins to pay. Under Medicare, you have no maximum on out-of-pocket expenses. Therefore, a Medicare supplement is a must.

While going through all the various costs of Medicare in detail is beyond the scope of this book, you should be aware of the current premium costs as of 2020. You should also familiarize yourself with the other costs you will pay in addition to premiums and deductibles.

PART B base minimum premium of $144.60

PLUS

- Premiums paid to private insurers for supplemental coverage
- Contributions to employer-sponsored retiree health plan OR
- Standalone prescription drug plan + Medigap policy OR

Medicare Advantage plan

PLUS

- Income-related monthly adjustment amount (IRMAA) for Part B and Part D, if applicable—can increase depending on income.

Medicare Enrollment

Yet another misconception about Medicare is that when you turn 65, it automatically begins. If you are already receiving Social Security when you turn 65, then it is automatic. If you have not turned on your Social Security by the time you turn 65, then you *must* enroll in Medicare three months before your 65th birthday. You sign up through the Social Security Administration either online at www.socialsecurity.gov or by calling the Social Security office at (800) 772-1213.

If you fail to enroll in Medicare during an enrollment period, you could end up paying a penalty when you do. There are two enrollment periods of which you should be aware.

The Initial Enrollment Period begins three months prior to your 65th birthday. It is for people who are signing up at age 65. This enrollment period lasts for seven months, but you must enroll sometime during that three-month period prior to your 65th birthday if you want to be covered on Day 1 of turning 65.

When you turn 65, if you are part of a group plan through your employer and that group plan covers twenty or more people, you can sign up later. This is called the Special Enrollment Period. Be sure to sign up for Medicare prior to your group coverage ending so you have no gap in coverage. If you enroll at some point during the seven-month period after your coverage ends, you should avoid late enrollment penalties.

There is also a General Enrollment Period which extends from January 1 – March 31 of each year. If you enroll during this time, your coverage will begin on July 1st. You may also be subject to enrollment penalties.

Supplemental Insurance

As you can see, there are a lot of out-of-pocket costs you are responsible for while on Medicare. Therefore, supplemental insurance is so very important. Plan on shopping supplemental insurance many months prior to the date your Medicare coverage begins so you are covered when your Medicare Starts.

Medigap insurance is designed to cover what Medicare does not. It is important to remember that if you sign up for Medigap insurance during either the Initial Enrollment or Special Enrollment periods, you will not be denied for health reasons. There is a standardization among policies, so pay attention to service and price when shopping.

Medicare Advantage Plans are available through private insurers. Often, these plans offer extra services such as vision and Medigap insurance. These companies contract with Medicare and handle all care under Parts A and B. They also usually offer a Part D drug plan as well.

Social Security

For most Americans, Social Security benefits represent a significant portion of their overall retirement income in the latter twenty years of their life. Planning when to turn it on may be one of the most critical decisions you will make.

Remember—Social Security provides a lifetime income that will not decline and continues to incorporate annual "COLA" or cost of living adjustments. COLA is tied to a certain measurement of inflation. Social Security may also provide a "survivor benefit" to both spouses, and even ex-spouses (if they were married for over ten years).

You can see how a wrong decision could result in tens or hundreds of thousands of dollars in lost income. There are several factors you should consider in making this decision.

- How much have you contributed over your lifetime?
- How is the status of your and your spouse's health?
- What are your entitled benefits at age 62, Full Retirement Age and at age 70?
- What other streams of income from various sources such as pensions, annuities, or investments (both qualified and non-qualified) are available to you and your spouse?

I was giving a seminar one evening on Social Security and a woman attending was amazed to discover that she was indeed, entitled to her deceased ex-husband's benefit. She was a woman with limited resources and had turned her Social Security on early. She was receiving less than $900/month. To further compound the problem, she was only working part time and barely getting by.

A few months later, she stopped by my office to talk to me for a few minutes. She immediately burst into tears and explained that she had just received her ex-husband's first monthly benefit which was about $2,000 more than her own. With the additional $24,000, her stress and anxiety had decreased significantly.

Her tears were no longer those of despair, but of gratitude. What she learned about Social Security that night had an impact on the rest of her life. Although she did not have the assets to become a client, she presented me with a box of Whitman chocolates from her local drug store in appreciation. I savored every chocolate in that box. This is just one example of how a little bit of planning and knowledge can significantly impact your life for years to come.

The biggest decision surrounding Social Security is when to take it. There are generally two schools of thought on this. There are those who believe applying for benefits as early as possible is the way to go—get as much as they can as soon as they can. Others choose to delay benefits if possible until age 70 so they can maximize the amount they will be paid each month.

If you are married, it is best to base your decision on your combined lifetime benefits. Let us say, you are the primary breadwinner and you decide to take your benefits early. If you die before your spouse, your spouse will get your reduced benefit for the rest of their life. Remember, when you choose to start Social Security early, you pay for it in the form of reduced benefits for the rest of your and your spouse's life.

On the other hand, let us say, you're still working and don't need to take your benefits, so you don't use Social Security until 70 years of age. If you predecease your spouse, they will receive your maximized benefit for the rest of their life.

Figuring out spousal combined lifetime benefits can be complicated. However, with potentially tens to hundreds of thousands of dollars on the line, it is well worth the time and energy you devote to the decision. It is best to talk to your financial advisor or reach out to me at www.jaylevyplanning.net to obtain some guidance.

Applying for Social Security

You can apply for Social Security in three ways. You can apply online at www.socialsecurity.gov. However, if you are applying for survivor benefits, at the time of this writing, you can not apply for them online. Another option is to call the Social Security Administration at (800) 772-1213. You can also apply at your local Social Security office. Use the office locator on the Social Security website for the address of your local office as well as directions and hours.

To avoid frustration, be sure to have the following documents with you:

- Social Security number
- Name at birth
- Date and place of birth
- Citizenship status
- The beginning and ending dates of each period of active-duty service if service occurred before 1968
- Whether you receive or expect to receive a pension or annuity based on employment with the federal government or one of its state or local subdivisions
- Current marital status and spouse's name, date of birth and Social Security number
- The names, dates of birth and Social Security numbers (if known) of any former spouses

- The dates and places of each marriage and for marriages that have ended—how and when they ended
- Names of any unmarried children under age 18
- The name and address of each employer for the last two years
- Information about self-employment
- Estimated earnings for the last year and this year and next year if application is made between September and December
- If you are within three months of turning 65, whether you want to enroll in Medicare Part B
- Bank account numbers for direct deposit

**From Horsesmouth: The Baby Boomer's Guide to Social Security*

Your amount of income determines if and how your Social Security benefits are taxed. This includes not only earned income but also income you will receive from pensions, investments* and municipal bonds. You will want to talk to a tax advisor, so you have clarity on all tax ramifications.

Retirement Accounts

At this writing, major changes are occurring in Washington D.C. The SECURE Act became law on Dec. 20, 2019. It includes major changes that could affect those in retirement, as well as their heirs.

The age at which you must start taking your required minimum distribution or RMD was raised from 70.5 to 72 years old. Another major change was the elimination of the stretch provision. This basically allowed non-spousal beneficiaries (namely your children) to "stretch" inherited qualified accounts over their remaining lifetime table.

Since the goal of the government was to collect taxes on this type of investment account sooner rather than later, the inherited benefit must be dispersed (with taxes due if it is a non-Roth account) within ten years of the inherited benefit. This means that a child must, by the end of the tenth year, take all the inheritance. They can do it either over some period during this time or wait and take the lump amount on the 3,650th day (and pay whatever the going individual tax rate is on such an amount).

There were some generally positive changes on the 401(k) side. The most noteworthy change is the easing of oversight by an employer to incorporate annuity-based insurance products as part of the investment lineup from which employees can select. The goal of this is to make it easier for participants to choose an investment that provides a guaranteed source of income upon retirement that is insured against potential market downturns.

An analysis of the holistic and financial aspects of our financial planning will determine at what point a stream of income from a qualified account will begin—either prior to the required RMD date or after. Your need for income from this source and potential tax consequences will determine when and how much income from a qualified account is utilized.

Pension and annuities provide an income stream that is important to the financial planning process. This will be one of the factors considered when determining how much and when you use other liquid assets.

Examine how much you will have coming in after-tax from all your income sources—Social Security, pensions, and annuities. Match your income sources to your fixed expenses and any identifiable discretionary expenses you anticipate. You do not necessarily have to access any of these income streams until you are ready.

Keep in mind that you benefit in higher monthly income from Social Security and annuities the longer you wait. Depending on your personal profile, it may make more financial sense to tap into other qualified or non-qualified holdings for covering these expenses while guaranteed income streams are delayed maximizing your payouts.

An mentioned in previous chapters, Social Security provides an 8% annual increase in your monthly income benefit for every year you wait to collect from Full Retirement Age until age 70.[86] As part of your retirement planning, we use mortality tables and your current health history to determine if delaying outweighs the benefit of turning on a reduced but earlier income stream.

Do not forget about inflation and its effect on fixed expenses. It is important to have clarity on which income streams have a COLA (Social Security) and which do not (pensions). Annuities can vary greatly in their potential for monthly income increases over your lifetime. Once you're clear on what your retirement assets will provide in the way of income streams, you can

[86] "What are Delayed Social Security Credits and How Do They Work." *AARP*. Accessed February 17, 2020. https://www.aarp.org/retirement/social-security/questions-answers/delayed-retirement-credits/

determine any "gap" that may exist between your guaranteed income streams and other additional income that may be needed to support your expected lifestyle

There are many different methods for addressing this gap. One of the more popular ones is called the "bucket strategy," which separates your assets into time, age, or any combination of related phases. These phases can either be stand-alone or work in synchronicity with each other to provide for your liquidity needs over your lifetime.

Regardless of what distribution method you choose, the primary goal is to avoid outliving your income in retirement. When utilizing the bucket strategy, we divide your assets into three-, five-, or nine-year buckets. Keep in mind that no process can guarantee with 100% certainty that you will not outlive your income. However, having a plan in place that can synchronize your income and annual distribution requirements provides a greater probability of success than just "shooting from the hip."

As an example, I have outlined a three-bucket strategy that continually moves assets between buckets during one's lifetime rather than just letting each bucket completely deplete itself.

Bucket #1: This bucket is designed to provide three to five years of liquid or near liquid assets. This bucket can include cash, money markets, one- to five-year laddered bonds and/or CD holdings. These assets once liquidated (after-tax) should adequately cover a three- to five-year period of estimated expenses. Your expense estimates should be reviewed each year as health, leisure, or family obligations arise.

Bucket #2: This bucket will hold assets such as annuities (if not turned on beforehand to generate income), laddered intermediate bond holdings with a five- to ten-year maturity. Equities can be added to this bucket to create an intermediate asset allocation. Overall, these types of holdings may be consistent with an asset allocation strategy of perhaps 30/70 or 40/60 mix of stocks to bonds.

Bucket #3: This bucket would be appropriate for a moderate or balanced asset allocation mix of 50/50 or 60/40. This bucket typically carries the highest risk/reward potential. Assets from this bucket can flow into the first or second buckets when its returns have exceeded some predetermined percentage such as 6% or

8%. Alternatively, when this bucket experiences negative or less than a predetermined target rate of return, assets should remain in place, so they have time to recover.

By having a certain percentage of your assets still invested for growth, you have an opportunity to benefit from long-term rates of return that keep pace with inflation. This type of strategy can significantly improve your chance of not outliving your income over a twenty-five- to forty-year retirement period. The advantage of continually moving assets between buckets when markets experience an annual return more than your pre-determined number, is that the other buckets are refilled.

Also, when the markets are down, risk is reduced because you are relying solely on Bucket #1 to cover expenses. Buckets #2 and #3 go untouched, which allows them to recover and grow when markets rebound.

It is important to reiterate that when it comes to taking distributions, no one strategy is considered perfect. Income versus spending always rules the day. If income declines for any reason, you must be prepared to adjust spending accordingly. Otherwise, even the best long-term strategy may be compromised permanently.

This is the resounding theme of this book. Plan as early as possible and periodically adjust your plan to the constant change that life throws at you. Honestly access your lifestyle to assess how long and healthy you could be living into your golden age.

Chapter 7 Action Steps

1. In this stage of life, the retirement plane is landing for you. Keeping in line with the airline metaphor, you may be arriving at your destination or realize that this is not a direct flight, just a temporary layover on your life journey. Medicare filings are required even if you may be continuing to work and utilize company medical plans. You are eligible for Social Security benefits (early, FRA, or perhaps delaying taking advantage of credits). Most retirement investments should have been accumulated prior to this point.

2. Some form of distribution plan should be established by first matching after-tax income streams against fixed expenses to determine how much you will have to dip into what you have accumulated. This may be in the form of some version of the bucket strategy or an alternative strategy for distribution. Your distribution plan should include when and how much you will have to pull from non-

qualified and qualified sources (401Ks, IRAs, etc.). Also, if you have utilized a Roth or have been doing Roth conversions of qualified investments, you will have to factor in when those assets will be distributed relative to the other investments you have accumulated. There is not necessarily a correct strategy as each one is based on individual need, tax rates (both federal and state), and the goal for those assets. Those who wish to leave their wealth to their children and those who want to leave a charitable legacy for some, or all their wealth will require very different strategies.

CHAPTER 8

Preservation of Assets, Quality of Life, & Your Legacy

As we head into our final chapter, which essentially covers planning for the last phase of your journey, it is important to remember everyone approaches this stage of life differently. Such planning is largely dependent on your physical and mental health, as well as the general outlook of life you carry with you into these later years.

Your physical, mental, and emotional state are all intricately connected. Even if you have taken good care of yourself, genetics and family history may impact you. In some cases, your physical health can significantly impact your mental and emotional state. The opposite can also be true. Your mental or emotional state can affect your physical health. I have seen cases where years of stress and anxiety over financial issues have taken a toll on a person's physical health.

Depression and general melancholy can also be a real threat as you age. If you are in reasonably good health as you age, you may find yourself attending more funerals than birthday parties as friends and family die more frequently. The more active you are, the more you may be able to insulate yourself from physical and mental issues, but you still must be able to survive loss as you age.

The human mind is wired for story, and I know from experience that stories stick with people far more than facts and figures. This last chapter is important, and I want it to stick with you, so I am going to end with a few stories. In the introduction of this book, I shared the unfortunate tale of my sister Donna's journey—one that started with such promise only to end with self-inflicted misfortune. In this last chapter, I would like to briefly share the stories of three other family members whose decisions have impacted me and the lives of those to whom I am closest.

I will begin with my father. Richard Levy was the son in a broken marriage during the Great Depression. My grandmother, who died at the age of 49 from cancer, was a fiercely independent woman. Despite her drive, at the age of 13, my father was expected to contribute whatever income he could. They owned a boat, so my father earned income for the family by taking people for excursions on the water around Rockport, MA.

Although he had to mature at a young age, he also had the good fortune of attending Boston Latin School. This provided him with a top-notch education and years later, he earned an engineering degree from MIT.

After serving in WWII as a naval submarine base commander, he settled down with my mother and their four children in Portsmouth, NH. He wanted to be his own boss, so he started an auto parts (Western Auto) business while also investing in real estate apartments and commercial properties.

While working as a self-proclaimed successful "slum lord," he entered politics as a moderate conservative and served on Portsmouth's City Council and moved onto the New Hampshire House of Representatives. During his political years he espoused libertarian views on keeping government small and staying out of people's personal affairs. With Portsmouth leaning in a more fiscally liberal direction during those years, he had no shortage of enemies.

While being extremely intelligent, he was not what I would describe as a warm and fuzzy man. He felt it his duty to debate with everyone concerning business, taxes, and the U.S. Constitution. Although most people respected him, he was not always enjoyable to be around—especially at social gatherings.

His father's abandonment greatly influenced his dysfunctional views on family. He made it perfectly clear on many occasions that he believed "children should be seen and not heard." This was the price we paid to have a roof over our heads and plentiful food on the table.

He also dictated the finances. I am certain that from an early age, he kept spreadsheets on all income and expenses. He developed the philosophy that the only good debt was that which could generate a measurable income stream. Buying things like expensive homes, cars, vacations, clothes, and anything else you can think of was immediately squashed. The only missteps with the expense planning process seemed to be in children. Although I cannot speak to his mindset regarding my three older siblings, I certainly was not a planned addition. This has been confirmed by just about every member of my family dating back to before I was born.

Although having a good handle on his family's finances, like many in his generation, my father had no focus on health whatsoever. Beginning in childhood and continuing with his years in the Navy, his true passion was always boating. He loved to pilot his boats either out on the ocean or up at Lake Winnipesaukee around Alton Bay, NH. Unfortunately, this was his only pleasure and he ate his way from svelte sailor in the 1930s and 40s to a significantly overweight man by the time the 1960s and I was born.

At the age of 55, he eventually decided to let others manage his businesses and real estate and semi-retire to Florida. Having few options at the age of 14, I moved to Key West with my parents in the early 1970s. My father got into a condo development and management partnership, which continued to keep him busy until age 62. That six- to seven-year stretch may have the best years of his life. He felt very little stress (Key West had that effect on people back then). He earned significant income in addition to his NH interests, and was surrounded by water.

Then he made the monumental and (I believe) poor choice to move from Key West to Fort Myers, where my two brothers had established law practices. Other than making some additional real estate investments along with tracking his prior holdings, he really had no life, passions, or hobbies. He spent whatever time he could with his two sons and waited for others (including myself) to come visit.

I remember these years as painful. Visiting him meant subjecting yourself to being lectured on how you should be living your life, debating politics, or being constantly lectured on the Constitution. These visits certainly were not fun or enjoyable and sometimes were intolerable. Although he would have still had another fifteen to twenty years of life, he became something which every person fears, *irrelevant*.

Therefore, it's so important that your planning is holistic in nature. It is critical to your retirement success that you not only consider finances but also the emotional and social aspects of retirement. These are areas you want to prepare for just as diligently as the financial aspects of your planning. They become increasingly more important as you age because they can significantly impact your quality of life.

My father, from a purely financial perspective certainly followed a proper financial planning process. He lived within his means and only incurred debt that was generally considered "good debt" because it was borrowed to purchase income-producing assets. In general, he avoided taking on huge risks. However, by remaining so conservative throughout his life, he missed out on a few wildly successful investments such as nursing homes and large apartment complexes.

In his later years, he lost a significant amount of money due to the bankruptcy of a Florida bank in which he held significant bond holdings. Other than those missteps, he diligently followed a financial planning process but missed the holistic aspects of the process. To be fair, back in his day, holistic planning was not even a thought.

My father focused almost exclusively on what he was "retiring from" (involvement in city and state politics, managing his business, real estate holdings, and lending activities). Had he considered what he was retiring "with" or "to," he would have been far better prepared for the last third of his life.

He spent the latter part of his life trying to control his children's lives with a balance sheet. He never realized that staying active was enjoyable and would have been life-sustaining for him. Instead, he left everything so he and my mother could enjoy the warmth of Florida only to experience the coldness of an empty, sad life.

My father's story represents one extreme that was no doubt, influential in molding my perspective. In many respects, it prompted me to author this book. Although my father did everything right financially, he did not die a happy man.

Contrast that with the story of my father-in-law, Les Horsager, who took a far more holistic path in retirement. Les and my mother-in-law, Linda brought up three children in a warm and loving environment. During his career with Prudential, Les moved his family to different zip codes numerous times over his children's lives. While this meant long term childhood relationships would never be established, the kids handled the moves without too much difficulty. Because of the frequent uprooting, Linda gave up her teaching career to dedicate herself to being a full-time mother. Eventually however, after Les moved the family to Prudential's corporate headquarters in Newark, NJ, she entered local politics, running successfully to serve on the Seabright, NJ city council.

Interestingly, Les would say that while the money was good, it was not great until the last fifteen years of his forty-year career with Prudential. Instead, what really drove him was his love of agriculture and the people with whom he interacted both in the field and within the company. It was obvious from the first time I met Les that he had a sincere interest in people, regardless of who they were or what they did. He was just at ease talking to wait staff at a restaurant as he was being interviewed by on television by Harry Reasoner for a *60 Minutes* segment involving litigation between farmers in Indiana and Prudential.

In fact, his life can best be summed up in an excerpt from his obituary, written by his son Jeff.

Leslie Grant Horsager died peacefully on February 28, 2017 at his home in Indio, California. Les is survived by his loving wife of 57 years, Linda Johnson Horsager, his children, grandchildren, and siblings. Born May 31, 1937 in LaMoure, ND, Les was proud of his North Dakota birthplace and his childhood home near Verndale, Minnesota. Although born into modest means, Les achieved success in his career yet remained humble throughout his life. Les graduated from the University of Minnesota in 1961 and immediately started teaching high school in Walnut Grove, MN. Two years later, Les changed vocations and started his 34-year career with Prudential Insurance making real estate loans and later investing in real estate for "Pru." He often said the secret to his career was to "hire good people and get out of their way."

Although very successful in his professional life, he took even greater joy in the growth and development of his children, grandchildren, nieces, and nephews. He loved sharing his network of friends and acquaintances with all of those around him. Maintaining friendships and nurturing new ones was a favorite pastime. Whether it be taking fishing or hunting trips, hosting, or attending reunions, or golfing, playing cards and travelling with close friends, staying in contact with those around him was one of his great joys in life. His retirement home, Birchview on Long Lake, provided a home-away-from-home for his family and many, many good friends.

Birchview was a wonderful setting for gathering and catching up with those he loved, and it enabled "Papa" to spend extended time with his beloved grandchildren.

Les was a generous, gregarious, caring, and loving husband, father, grandfather, uncle, and friend. Respecting his desire to have the celebration of his life close to the places he loved best, a memorial service will take place at 1:30 p.m. on May 27, 2017 at Calvary Lutheran Church in Park Rapids, Minnesota.

Les and my dad could not have approached their life or their finances more differently. My father was consumed with money and held it over his family's head throughout his life. Did he enjoy life and everything he worked for? I believe he may have had fleeting glimpses of enjoyment, but he certainly did not live the rich, full, and rewarding life that my father-in-law did. Therefore, holistic planning is so very important.

World renown psychologist, Dr. Martin Seligman studied human well-being extensively and identified five factors that facilitate it. This is called the PERMA theory of well-being: Positive Emotion, Engagement, Relationships, Meaning and Accomplishment.[87]

---

[87] "PERMA Theory of Well-Being and PERMA Workshops." *Positive Psychology Center, University of Pennsylvania.* Accessed March 4, 2020.

The "with" is not about assets. It is more about what your work-life represented to you. If your career did not provide you with positive emotions, didn't generate an engaged mentality, limited or reduced your ability to maintain positive relationships, didn't provide any deep rooted meaning, and didn't generate any type of measurable personal accomplishment, then chances are you're going to have to live with these same issues in retirement as well.

The "to" is not exclusively about assets either. Rather, it is about analyzing the PERMA components and where you stand with each one as you enter retirement. Anticipating changes in PERMA factors are paramount to a happy and successful retirement. In the case of my father and Les, they traveled very different paths in retirement.

My father was anything but positive in his semi-retired life. While he dabbled with his investments and lending activities, his primary focus was to influence his children's lives by lecturing, educating, criticizing, and judging to control his grown children. I believe his reasons for this behavior can be traced back to a fear of becoming irrelevant which was exactly what he became in his later years. With his social network relatively non-

---

https://ppc.sas.upenn.edu/learn-more/perma-theory-well-being-and-perma-workshops

existent after retirement, his children were his one remaining audience. To ensure they remained geographically close, he simply used the allure of his personal balance sheet as bait. Failure to follow his way of living your life usually meant criticism and the threat of being cut off from any inheritance.

He essentially failed the PERMA test on all accounts. He and my mother did have some happy times. However, the lack of engagement, minimal social relationships, little real meaning (either religious or spiritual) and nothing noteworthy regarding accomplishments (other than talking about the "past") meant his well-being in retirement was limited to non-existent.

Although their children were of primary importance to both my parents and my in-laws, the similarities ended there. My folks wanted to maintain significant control over their kid's lives even beyond the grave. My in-laws on the other hand believed that their obligation was to lovingly raise their children to be well educated, and ultimately self-reliant as they proceeded through their lives. There were no promises of inheritances. Their main goal was to enjoy and participate in their children's and grandchildren's lives. There was relatively little control, judging, or criticism when it came to family.

Les and Linda built their dream retirement home in Park Rapids, near where they each grew up in Minnesota.

However, it was their summer home that was the special place where grandchildren would spend each of their summers together. To this day, it is still a magical place filled with memories of the past and pleasures of the present.

At the time of his retirement at age 60, Les had a healthy grasp of PERMA factors. Both he and Linda had been extremely positive on a day-by-day basis in their work lives, which carried over into retirement. They made the effort to stay in touch and constantly engage with friends and family. Watching the continual growth and evolution of their children and grandchildren was extremely meaningful to both. Their religious and spiritual life also held great meaning for them.

Les was taken from his family and friends by cancer in 2017. Everyone who had the privilege of knowing this exceptional man considered themselves truly blessed, and we are all still fortunate to have my mother-in-law very active and an important part of our lives.

My last story belongs to Renee Levy, my aunt and founder of State Street Discount Inc., a 65-year old high-end appliance, TV, and home audio business in Portsmouth, NH. Renee's retirement story is very different from my father's and father-in-law's. Both men, having the financial means to do so, retired around the age of 60. Each knew what they were *"retiring from,"* my father from politics, investing and managing real estate, and Les from the daily travel and corporate pressures of working for Prudential. However, Les knew what he was retiring *"with and to,"* and my father did not.

Unlike my father and Les, my Aunt Renee never retired. With the assistance of her brother-in-law, (my father) she opened her business in 1955 with the same financial fears anyone in her position would have—probably more so since she was a woman. She worked seven days a week to build a reputable retailing business that has persevered and grown for over six decades. Large box retailers such as Woolworths, Circuit City, Sears, and others have come and gone while State Street Discount Inc. proved to be the little business that could. Renee carried the torch until her son assumed leadership in the late 1980s. Did that mean she retired? Not Renee! Instead of heading off into some retirement sunset, this thin, red headed, impeccably dressed, bejeweled woman still opens her business seven days a week, fifty-two weeks a year.

Money has not been an issue for my aunt for decades. Why then, does she still open her company every day at 8 a.m. and is always the first one in? Nothing demonstrates the value of holistic planning better than Renee. The business still provides the primary venue for adding meaning in her life. It is her lifeblood and despite age-related aches and pains, it is still her happy place that gives meaning and purpose to her life.

While Renee has one child who oversees the business, she has no grandchildren. She can see her son both within the store and outside it for a daily afternoon walk together. While others may view such a lifestyle as too repetitive or demanding for a woman 87 years old, Renee knows she would be bored to death and extremely unhappy with any other lifestyle. It works for her.

If you retain nothing else from this final chapter, please get this. Financial planning early and often is an essential factor in your ability to retire and in the type of lifestyle you retire to. However, it is only one piece of the retirement puzzle. Holistic planning is what ultimately determines your happiness and well-being in retirement. Have a firm grasp on not only what you are retiring from, but also what you are retiring with and to. The more clarity you have on this, the happier and more successful your retirement will be.

Chapter 8 Action Steps

1. Start the holistic retirement planning process by performing a deep self-assessment of yourself. From Chapters 6 and 7 you will recall using the "PERMA" acronym which stands for:

   Positive Emotions
   Engagement
   Relationships
   Meaning
   Acknowledgment or Accomplishment

2. This transitions your thinking from what you are retiring "from" (which not only includes employment and finances to date, but also current relationships, geographical locations, current passions, meaning or spiritual, etc.) to deeply contemplating what you are retiring "with" (at the moment) and retiring "to" (what you want going forward in the future).

Epilogue

As this book reaches its final editing phase, it is imperative that I mention where this country—actually, the entire globe stands regarding the COVID-19 and its potential economic impact. Heading into April of 2020, the world is experiencing a non-military panic not seen since the Spanish Flu back in 1918.

When we look back over history, the first World War was terrifying in terms of mass destruction. However, that level of destruction was ultimately surpassed in World War II some twenty years later. Regardless of which side you were on, there was always an identifiable enemy.

The Great Depression was an applicable name for that time in our history. I believe that 2020 will pale in terms of economic impact compared to the Great Depression but that is remains to be seen. What 1929 did not have was the overwhelming panic associated with a worldwide health crisis.

Only in hindsight will historians assess whether the closing of everyday Americana was beneficial and ultimately worth the economic loss. That at this moment is incalculable. The 2020 health pandemic is a life-changing event for everyone around the globe. Initial cost estimates of impending unemployment, business insolvencies, and questionable survival of entire industries, is staggering.

With that said, I have asked myself repeatedly with each passing day, if a book I started more than two years ago with no information to speak of on the Coronavirus (*or* the beer) still had relevancy. Considering the plight of individuals, small and large businesses and even governments, I am convinced the answer is a resounding yes!

The current crisis is certainly different than the 2007-2009 Great Recession, which was primarily caused by greed and a self-destructive collateralized mortgage financial debacle. Today's crisis is centered around a health pandemic leading to potential significant economic and financial ramifications.

It is certainly no fault of workers, businesses, or anyone else when the government orders shutdowns—cutting off the lifeblood of revenue and income that fuels this country's economic engine. No, this is not anyone's fault and yet...the principals of planning in this book could be viewed as a series of a long-term precautions. My hope is that these principles can at least soften the impact of a "trigger event," such as one we are currently experiencing with COVID-19.

As challenging as it is, those who were able to build sufficient emergency funds for a least a few months if not a year avoided an immediate financial crisis. Fixed and discretionary expenses do not disappear when revenue or wages suddenly do. It greatly reduces stress when you do not have to worry if you can afford next month's rent or next week's groceries. This is just one of the many benefits of planning.

Planning has no emotion. It is cold, calculating, and requires discipline. Delaying some degree of short-term gratification to build toward a long-term goal—whether it be an emergency fund, retirement, or some combination—is perhaps the greatest human disciple of all. It is because of this principled framework that I believe this book is more critical than it was when I first conceived of it a couple years ago.

It is my hope that this book has not only given you a 30,000-foot-view of your financial life cycle, as well as the tools and strategies you need to either begin or fine-tune your holistic planning. Although I guided you on a journey through a financial lifetime in this book, there are some key themes I would like to drive home before I close.

First, it is never too early or too late to begin planning for your life and your retirement. If you fail to plan, life has a way of planning for you. If you are starting late with your planning, remember that starting is always better than not, regardless of age.

Remember that your children's financial education comes primarily from you. Do not depend on the educational system whether private or public to properly educate them on money and finances. When you and your family are working through the college planning process, partner with your child to make it a teachable moment. Children learn far more from your actions than they do your words, so do your best to make everyday a teachable moment for them. It is those teachable moments that prepare them for life.

Money and finances will be a constant for the rest of their lives. It is your job to educate them in the lessons that will serve them well throughout adulthood.

Approach your planning holistically. It should include a financial component as well as the non-financial that includes health, happiness, and well-being factors. This is how you holistically plan for a truly balanced life.

Know yourself—your strengths and your limitations and learn to work with them. As distasteful as it might seem now, bite the bullet and create a budget. Everyone needs one—regardless of income. The sooner you become adept at this, the faster your will take control of your finances.

Begin to save and invest from your very first paycheck. Contributing to your employer retirement plan is one of the easiest and most effective ways of saving. Your contributions are deducted from your paycheck before you even see it, which requires far less discipline on your part. As soon as possible, contribute enough to maximize your employer match if they offer one. Also as soon as possible, max out what you can contribute.

By doing this, you are not only maximizing the free money you receive from your employer through their match, but whatever you contribute grows tax-deferred until you withdraw. That is a heck of a deal because your money grows exponentially faster when Uncle Sam is not taking his cut every year. You will be amazed at how quickly your 401(k), 403(b), and IRA accounts can grow over the years when no taxes are taken out annually.

Have a firm grasp on your income and expenses now and as you approach retirement. Understand the difference between fixed and discretionary expenses and use guaranteed income streams to cover fixed expenses in retirement. Get the advice of a financial advisor before you make Social Security and Medicare decisions. Both are very important to your retirement success.

My wish is that you live a long and prosperous life and enjoy many happy, healthy years in retirement. I can be reached at (603) 512-1911, by emailing:

jaylevyplanning@gmail.com or by visiting **www.jaylevyplanning.net** for complimentary planning tools you can utilize to get started. I am always here to help. Best of luck!

Bibliography

"7 Steps to a Richer Retirement." *Kiplinger's*. Accessed January 28, 2020. https://store.kiplinger.com/7-steps-to-retirement.html.

"7 Ways Millennials Are Changing The Healthcare Industry (And What It Means To You)." Accessed January 19, 2020. https://www.teamhfa.com/news/insights/7-ways-millennials-are-changing-healthcare-industry.

"2019 Least Stressful Jobs." Accessed November 30, 2019. https://www.careercast.com/jobs-rated/least-stressful-2019?page=9/.

"A Couple Retiring in 2018 Would Need an Estimated $280,000 to Cover Health Care Costs in Retirement, Fidelity® Analysis Shows." *Fidelity.* April 19, 2018. https://www.fidelity.com/about-fidelity/employer-services/a-couple-retiring-in-2018-would-need-estimated-280000.

"A Primer for Financial Literacy for Kids." *National Financial Educator's Council*. Accessed March 20, 2020. https://www.financialeducatorscouncil.org/financial-literacy-for-kids/.

Adamczyk, Alicia. "The Salary You Need To Buy a Home in 10 of The Largest Cities in The U.S." *CNBC.* October 10, 2019. https://www.cnbc.com/2019/10/10/the-salary-you-need-to-buy-a-house-in-large-us-cities.html.

Adams, Jane Meredith. "Raising a Compassionate Child." *Parenting.* Accessed March 17, 2020. https://www.parenting.com/child/raising-a-compassionate-child/.

Amadeo, Kimberly. "The Rising Cost of Health Care by Year and It's Causes." *The Balance*. Updated February 28, 2020. https://www.thebalance.com/causes-of-rising-healthcare-costs-4064878

Blay, Joyce. "Worker Health Premiums Now Topping $20K Year." *Financial Advisor Magazine.* October 1, 2019.

Carpenter, Julia. "Your Parents' Financial Advice is (Kind Of) Wrong." *Wall Street Journal*. September 13, 2019. https://www.wsj.com/articles/your-parents-financial-advice-is-kind-of-wrong-11568367000.

Desjardins, Jeff. "America's Growing Financial Literacy Problem." *Visual Capitalist.* October 28, 2018. https://www.visualcapitalist.com/americas-growing-financial-literacy-problem/.

Eaglesham, Jean, Jones, Coulte, Tobin, Michael Tobin. "Soaring Student Debt Opens Door To Relief Scams." *Wall Street Journal.* August 26, 2019.

Eisen, Ben, Roberts, Adrienne. “The Seven-Year Auto Loan; America’s Middle Class Can’t Afford Their Cara.” *Wall Street Journal.* October 1, 2019.

“Evaluating the Housing Market Since the Great Recession.” *Core Logic.* Accessed December 26, 2019. https://www.corelogic.com/downloadable-docs/core-logic-peak-totrough-final-030118.pdf.

Elkins, Kathleen. “29% of Americans Are Considered Lower Class - Here is How Much Money They Earn.” *CNBC.* September 28, 2019. https://www.cnbc.com/2019/09/28/how-much-the-american-lower-class-earns.html.

Findell, Elizabeth. “Homelessness Becomes More Visible In Austin, Sparking Political Clash.” *Wall Street Journal.* October 24, 2019. https://www.wsj.com/articles/homeless-becomes-more-visible-in-austin-sparking-political-clash-11571914802.

Floyd, Elaine. “Savvy Social Security Course.” *Horsesmouth.* 2020 Edition.

Goss, Stephen C. “The Financial Future of the Social Security Program.” *Social Security Office of Retirement and Disability Policy.* Accessed February 9, 2020. https://www.ssa.gov/policy/docs/ssb/v70n3/v70n3p111.html.

“Got Kids? 6 Ways to Manage Costs.” *Fidelity.* February 20, 2019. https://www.fidelity.com/learning-center/personal-finance/college-planning/managing-costs-raising-child.

Hass, David. "Retirement Trends of Baby Boomers." *Forbes*. September 3, 2019. https://www.forbes.com/sites/forbesfinancecouncil/2019/09/03/retirement-trends-of-baby-boomers/#4fa6a60d7378.

Harrison, David. "Historical Asset Boom Passes By Half of Families." *Wall Street Journal*. August 30, 2019. https://www.wsj.com/articles/historic-asset-boom-passes-by-half-of-families-11567157400.

Hinden, Steven. "How Much Does Early Retirement Reduce Benefits." *AARP*. Accessed February 9, 2020. https://www.aarp.org/work/social-security/info-04-2013/early-retirement-social-security-benefits.html.

Liu, Jennifer. "The Highest-Paying, Low-Stress Job in The U.S. Pays $208,000 a Year." *CNBC*. October 2, 2019. https://www.cnbc.com/2019/10/01/us-news-world-report-10-highest-paying-lowest-stress-jobs.html.

MacMillan, Amanda. "Happiness Linked to Longer Life. " *CNN*. Updated July 20, 2018. https://www.cnn.com/2011/10/31/health/happiness-linked-longer-life/index.html.

Mapes, Jeff. "Oregon Strikes Exclusive Single-Family Zoning But Effects May Take Years." *OPB*. July 3, 2019.

https://opb.org/news/article/oregon-single-family-zoning-law-effect-developers/.

Moore, Emily. "Highest Paid Careers of 2019." Posted on September 17, 2019. https://www.glassdoor.com/blog/highest-paying-jobs-2019/.

Muntikani, Lucia. "U.S. Housing Starts Rise, Single-Family Segment Still Weak." *Reuters.* December 18, 2018. https://www.reuters.com/article/us-usa-economy/u-s-housing-starts-rise-single-family-segment-remains-ewak-idUSKBN1OH1H8.

Parker, Tim. "The Cost of Raising a Child in America." *Investopedia*. Updated May 20, 2019. https://www.investopedia.com/articles/personal-finance/090415/cost-raising-child-america.asp

"PERMA Theory of Well-Being and PERMA Workshops." *Positive Psychology Center, University of Pennsylvania.* Accessed March 4, 2020. https://ppc.sas.upenn.edu/learn-more/perma-theory-well-being-and-perma-workshops/.

Probasco, Jim. "6 Social Security Changes in 2020." *Investopedia*. Updated January 24, 2020. https://www.ssa.gov/policy/docs/ssb/v70n3/v70n3p111.html/.

"Retirement Confidence Survey." *Employee Benefit Research Institute*. April 24, 2018.

https://www.ebri.org/docs/default-source/rcs/1_2018rcs_report_v5mgachecked.pdf?sfvrsn=e2e9302f_2/.

Ramakumar, Amrith. "Rising California Gasoline Prices Highlight Growing Divide in Us." *Wall Street Journal.* October 23, 2019. https://www.wsj.com/articles/rising-california-gasoline-prices-highlight-growing-divide-in-u-s-11571832001.

Rogers, Kristen. "U.S Teens Use Screens More Than Seven Hours a Day On Average—And That's Not Including School Work." *CNN*. October 29, 2019. https://www.cnn.com/2019/10/29/health/common-sense-kids-media-use-report-wellness/index.html/.

"Social Security Recipient to Worker Ratio." *Federal Budget in Pictures.* Accessed February 9, 2020. https://www.federalbudgetinpictures.com/social-security-recipient-worker-ratio/.

"Survey: Certified Divorce Financial Analysts Reveal The Leading Causes of Divorce." *Institute of Divorce Financial Analysts.* Accessed January 10, 2020. https://institutedfa.com/Leading-Causes-Divorce/.

"Survey of New Hampshire High Schools." *JumpStart Financial Smarts For Students, New Hampshire Coalition 2017.*

Tatham, Matt. "Auto Loan Debt Sets Record Highs." *Experian.* July 18, 2019.

https://www.experian.com/blogs/ask-experiamn/research/auto-loan-debt-study/.

"The Social Security Trust Fund Will Run Out of Money by 2035." *Barron's*. Accessed February 9, 2020. https://www.barrons.com/articles/social-security-deficit-reserves-check-benefits-payroll-tax-51555958282

"What are Delayed Social Security Credits and How Do They Work." *AARP*. Accessed February 17, 2020. https://www.aarp.org/retirement/social-security/questions-answers/delayed-retirement-credits/.

Xie, Stella Yifan, Li, Shandi and Wernau, Julie. "Young Chinese Spend Like Americans and Take on Worrisome Debt." *Wall Street Journal*. August 29, 2019. https://www.wsj.com/articles/young-chinese-spend-like-americansand-take-on-worrisome-debt-11567093953/.

"You're Probably Not Ready to Retire – Psychologically," *MarketWatch.* Accessed February 15, 2020. https://www.marketwatch.com/story/why-youre-probably-not-psychologically-ready-to-retire-2019-05-21/.

ABOUT THE AUTHOR

Jay Levy has been in the financial services and banking industries for over 30 years. As a Certified Financial Planner, he continues to work with individuals, multi-generational families and businesses regarding investments, retirement, estate, tax, and financial planning services. From 2017-2019, he has been voted the #1 Financial Planner in the "Best of The Seacoast" Annual survey by Seacoast Media Group for the past 3 years.

Jay has been a guest lecturer at various colleges including the University of New Hampshire and the F.W. Olin MBA School at Babson. He has also been involved in national politics serving as a Town Chair for Senator John

McCain's presidential campaign in 2008 and as the NH Financial Chair for Governor Tim Pawlenty's presidential campaign in 2010.

Jay has served on numerous Boards over the years. He currently serves on the Wentworth Douglass Hospital Foundation Board as Past Chair.

Jay and his wife Kelly live in the lovely, quaint town of Stratham, NH and are the proud parents of two sons Grant and Adam, each who reside near Boston, MA. Both, much to the delight of their parents, are gainfully employed and self-sufficient.

Made in the USA
Middletown, DE
26 July 2020

12978071R00139